BACK TAXES & TAX DEBT

A Consumer's Guide to Understanding
IRS Tax Debt and What Can Be Done About It

Donald E. Lowrey, Esq.

TaxLawyerOnline™

LAS VEGAS, NEVADA

Donald E. Lowrey
P.O. Box 750271
Las Vegas NV 89136
www.taxlawyeronline.net

Publisher's Note: Names, characters, places, and incidents are a product of the author's imagination. Locales and public names are sometimes used for atmospheric purposes. Any resemblance to actual people, living or dead, or to businesses, companies, events, institutions, or locales is completely coincidental.

Book Layout © 2014 BookDesignTemplates.com

This book is designed to provide accurate and authoritative information of a general nature in regard to the subject matter covered. It is not intended to provide specific legal advice to you. Use of this book in any format, or any communication by mail, e-mail, telephone or by other means, is not legal advice and does not create an attorney-client privilege. An attorney client relationship can only be created by an express agreement. We do not represent you until such time as we expressly accept your representation.

Back Taxes & Tax Debt/ Donald E. Lowrey. -- 1st ed.
ISBN 13: 978-0615995519 (Donald Lowrey)
ISBN-10: 0615995519

Dedicated to the hardworking, over regulated
and overtaxed people of the United States of America.
May you ever preserve your rights as free citizens.

*"Anyone may arrange his affairs so that his taxes shall be as
low as possible; he is not bound to choose that pattern which
best pays the treasury. There is not even a patriotic duty to
increase one's taxes.*

*Over and over again the Courts have said that there is
nothing sinister in so arranging affairs as to keep taxes as low
as possible. Everyone does it, rich and poor alike and all do
right, for nobody owes any public duty to pay more than the law
demands."*

—Judge Learned Hand

(1872 – 1961), Judge U.S. Court Of Appeals
In The Case Of Gregory v. Helvering 69 F. 2d 809
(2d Cir. 1934), Aff'd, 293 U.S. 465 (1935)

–If the IRS says you owe, this book is for you –

**This book is written for the average person
who does not have a tax background.**

The IRS is the largest collection organization in the world. You are its target. *This book* is:

- **Fundamental** to an understanding of how the IRS works and how its operations affect you.
- **Indispensable** to an understanding of what the IRS wants from you.
- **Essential** to an understanding *your rights* under the law.

Most tax problems do <u>not</u> require the services of a tax attorney.

However, time is not on your side. You must get on top of tax problems early. You may lose important rights, merely by the passage of time.

CONTENTS

CHAPTER ONE

INTRODUCTION

The IRS is the largest collection organization in the world. You are its target. *This book* is:

- **Fundamental** to an understanding of how the IRS works and how its operations affect you.
- **Indispensable** to an understanding of what the IRS wants from you.
- **Essential** to an understanding *your rights* under the law.

−If the IRS says you owe, this book is for you −

How to Read This Book − Skip Around!

This is *not* a book that you read from the front to the back. I have organized the chapters according to the tax issues that I commonly see in my law practice, e.g. my list of "frequently asked questions". Feel free to skip around to the chapters that are most closely related to your tax issue.

**This book is written for the average person
who does not have a tax background.**

Don't try to absorb everything at once. Put the book down and come back to it later.

Knowledge is Power

Fear of the IRS is natural. Knowledge empowers you. Knowledge takes away a natural fear of the unknown and gives you a tool to solve your tax problem. Whether you retain tax counsel or attempt to do it yourself, understanding the issue at hand gives you a great advantage.

Disclaimer

For the sake of full disclosure, we want you to know that the author is attorney who maintains a tax collection and tax dispute law practice TaxLawyerOnline™, a virtual law firm that provides tax matter legal services on-line at reduced fees. The information contained in this book is intended to be general information and is not intended to be specific legal advice or the rendering of legal services. If legal advice or assistance is required, the services of a competent professional should be sought. To learn more, visit:

www.taxlawyeronline.net

<u>You</u> Can Resolve Your Tax Case

– Most tax problems do not require the services of an attorney

Tax problems start out small, and like a cancer, grow over time. In the early stages you can resolve the problem yourself. You will find that the information in this book will assist you in dealing with the IRS.

Understanding

Sometimes an explanation is all you need. In this book we describe the processes and the means by which the IRS collects taxes. Perhaps more importantly, we talk about solutions to various tax problems. You may find that one or more solutions are applicable to you and your tax problem.

Case Studies and Examples

From time to time you will come across a case study. A case study is a short story about a taxpayer who has had problems with the IRS. Each case study is based on a real situation. However, because we maintain the confidentiality of clients, the names are fictional and some facts like the amount or location or other particulars may be changed from the actual case. If the name of a tax preparation service is mentioned, it is entirely fictional.

−A case study is short story that illustrates a tax problem

The short stories are intended to personalize information in a way that will be helpful to an understanding of the fundamental issues of your tax matter. The resolution of your tax case may have an entirely different result that the person(s) described in the case study. This because every tax case is different, and every tax case depends on the particular facts of the individuals.

It is my sincere hope that you will find this book both informative and helpful. Most tax problems do not require attorney services. With a little knowledge, you can resolve the problem.

Believe in yourself – *You've got this!*

Sincerely,
Donald Lowrey, JD LLM
Attorney at Law

CHAPTER TWO

MEET THE IRS

Administration

The first function of the Internal Revenue Service is to administer and regulate taxation at the federal level. The IRS is a part of the Administrative Branch of the federal government, falling under the Department of the Treasury. However, the laws that form our tax code come from Congress. Frequently Congress does not draft tax laws in detail. Rather Congress gives more general instructions and leaves it up to the IRS to draft the specifics. The IRS has to interpret the law and to do so, issues various regulations and other documents to provide guidance to taxpayers. In addition, Congress is responsible for providing funding for the IRS that ironically is paid for by the very taxes that it collects. This brings us to the second major function of the Internal Revenue Service, revenue collection.

Revenue Collection

Income Taxes

Income tax collection is the area that you are most likely to encounter an IRS notice. Everyone knows that you must file a tax return annually (with limited exceptions). The other side of the coin is payment of the tax due. These are separate and distinct from each other as you will see in other chapters. The IRS is the largest collection agency in the world. This is staggering when you think about all the various types of taxes that are applied, administered and collected by the IRS.

In this book, we are concerned only with income tax. Income tax is obviously, assessed on income. You may be surprised to know that income is not only money, but any tangible benefit received in any form and from any source. Of course, there are exceptions, deductions, credits and lots of special regulations to accommodate special interest groups.

There are other kinds of taxes that should be mentioned so that you will have a sense of the "big picture".

Excise Tax

An excise tax is a tax imposed on the consumption or use of certain products; the most common are gasoline and alcoholic beverages. There is federal excise tax which you may be familiar with; an 18 ½ cent tax on every gallon of gasoline. As of this writing, the federal excise tax on alcoholic beverages is $13.50 per gallon on distilled spirits and anywhere from a $1.07 to $3.40 per gallon on wine. Don't forget state excise taxes on top of the federal tax.

> *Interesting fact: 40% of what you pay for beer goes to taxes.*
> -Sarah Mimms, National Journal

Disguised Federal Taxes

The government also imposes taxes in ways that are not so obvious. For example, the service fee or entrance fee for a national park is a form of taxation even if it's not called a tax. Even the IRS hides taxes for certain services. If you want to start a non-profit corporation the law allows you to do so. The "but" is that the IRS charges $400 as a user fee to process your application – another way to tax you without calling it a tax. In short, anything that breathes, moves, lays in the ground or can be imagined is taxed in the United States one way or another.

Estate and Gift Tax

As you know that there is a federal tax on the estate of a deceased person and a tax on gifts made during the lifetime of the deceased. The tax doesn't kick in until the value of the estate or the amount of gifts is at a fairly high level. Even so, if it is your estate you may think this unfair. Why? You worked your entire life saving your money and wisely investing it. Along the way, you paid income tax on your wages, taxes on distributions of dividends from the corporations in which you invested. You paid capital gains tax on the growth of your investments. If you owned your own business, you paid income tax on what the business, through your worry, sweat and labor, earned. Everything in your estate has been taxed at least once and often several times. On your death, you get to pay tax again on what has already been taxed. Lucky you.

The Bureaucracy of Tax Law

To give you some idea of the size of the tax bureaucracy, below are some quotes from elected representatives:

"The Internal Revenue Code and regulations at up to 1 million words and is nearly 7 times the length of the Bible". *U.S. Representative John Hostettler (R-IN)*

"The income tax code and its associated regulations contain almost 5.6 million words— seven times as many words as the Bible. Taxpayers now spend about 5.4 billion hours a year trying to comply with 2500 pages of tax laws …”. *U.S. Representative Rob Portman (R-OH)*

Added to the tax code are administrative regulations and interpretations. Tax law is interpreted by Tax Court decisions, Treasury Regulations, the Internal Revenue Manual, Notices and Private Letter Rulings – each rule shading and further complicating the plain meaning of the laws passed by Congress. You get the idea; there is a lot of information to know. In a real sense, you have to know tax law to find the answer to a tax question. No wonder it is so difficult for the average person to get an answer to what seems like a simple question.

Total pages of federal tax rules

Total pages of federal tax rules (explanation of U.S. income tax code and regulations):

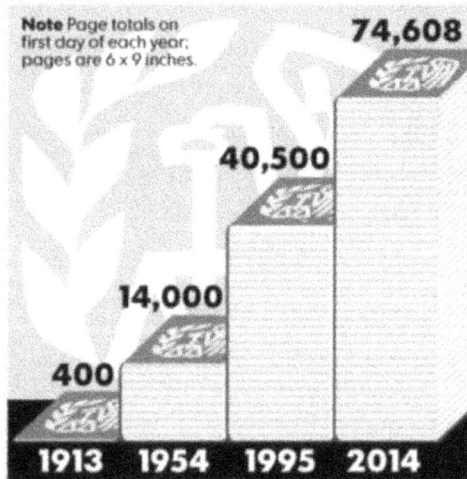

Note Page totals on first day of each year; pages are 6 x 9 inches.

Year	Total pages
1913	400
1954	14,000
1995	40,500
2014	74,608

Source Wolters Kluwer, CCH: 2014
ANNE R. CAREY AND PAUL TRAP, USA TODAY

If you are interested, the complete Internal Revenue Code is available for sale from the U.S. Government Printing Office. You can order only a portion of the law, as, for example, if you are only interested in that part relating to Partnership taxation. Caution, you will find that there will be lots of references to other parts. Pay attention, because those references define the meaning of a particular phrase or usage in the section you are reading.

CHAPTER THREE

IRS LETTERS AND NOTICES

The IRS automates routine task as much as possible. This means that the IRS generates millions of form letters to taxpayers every year. Some letters are more serious than others. In general, a letter from the IRS is a notice of disagreement or missing information. For example, if you fail to file an individual tax return the IRS will send you a form letter. If the IRS questions a deduction that you took on your tax return, it will send you a form letter.

Notices & Letters

If you receive a letter from the IRS, don't panic. Look carefully at the letter. The information that you want to know is the tax year and the type of tax (for most readers, this will be income tax). This is information that you need to know before you can determine why the IRS has contacted you.

  – *Examine each Notice carefully for the type of tax and the year in issue. Is the Notice a proposed adjustment, assessment or a balance due?*

Each letter notice contains instructions. Often the instructions are worded in bureaucratic language that can be difficult. Here's an approach that I suggest. Take each paragraph in the letter, one at a time, and make a note in the margin of the letter about the main purpose of that paragraph. This will help you turn an incomprehensible notice into something understandable.

Proposed Corrections

Some letters are correction letters. By that I mean the IRS has proposed a correction to your tax return. If you do nothing, then the IRS will make that change, and you may owe additional tax. I have found that taxpayers do nothing afte receiving a notice because they don't understand the notice.

Ignore these notices at your peril. If no response is made the correction becomes an assessment, and you will owe an additional tax caused by the change in your return. Don't be surprised by a tax bill following assessment.

Instead of doing nothing, compare the proposed correction with your tax return. Sometimes finding the proposed correction is easy. Every line of a tax return form is numbered sequentially. The line number is used to reference a particular entry on the tax form. Unfortunately, sometimes the IRS doesn't make it easy because the letter does not make a call out to a particular line item of your tax return.

– Reply in writing to any letter proposing an increase in tax. You will have better success at this stage than if you wait until after assessment.

Often the correction letter is not very helpful for another reason. If you don't already have a good understanding of how your taxes are calculated, it can be difficult to understand what caused the proposed change. Did the IRS receive another W-2 that you did not? Was the amount on your W-2 or 1099-MISC different from that reported by a third party to the IRS?

Do not let this discourage you. You can call the IRS and asked to have the proposed change explained. Be prepared when you make the call. Have a copy of your tax return, as you filed it, in front of you so that you see where the proposed changes are to occur.

If something doesn't look right to you, don't hesitate to question it. Ask questions. Also, if you paid someone to prepare your tax return, the preparer should explain the proposed changes to you without any additional fee. If there's a mistake, the paid preparer should correct the return for you and/or explain the entry to the IRS. We have included a chapter in this book about the role of paid tax preparers.

How to Read the IRS Notice or Letter

A correction of your tax return is only one of the many types of notices are letters that the IRS issues. It can be daunting to try to unravel the letter. I have included an illustration of a typical IRS notice at the end of this chapter. It has been marked up to show you how to decode it.

The IRS publishes on its web site a list of the code numbers and a short explanation. The list is too long to include in this book. The link to the code numbers, as of the writing of this book is:
http://www.irs.gov/Individuals/Understanding-Your-IRS-Notice-or-Letter.

The IRS does not publish all of its form letters on its web site. If you receive a letter that is not on the list, you will need to call the IRS and inquire. It is important to understand exactly the nature of the problem. You do not want to guess or put it off. Inaction can be costly, troublesome and could result in the loss of legal rights.

Department of the Treasury
Internal Revenue Service
Fresno, CA 93888-0025

The IRS Form #

The year about which
the IRS is writing you.

Is this your SSAN?

Notice	CP504
Tax Year	2010
Notice date	
Social Security number	
To contact us	Phone 1-800-829-0922
Page 1 of 4	

005320.896219
540

Name and address where notice was sent

IMPORTANT! This amount is only for the tax year stated on the notice. If you owe for more than one year, you need to add the amounts from other years.

Notice of intent to levy

Intent to seize your property or rights to property
Amount due immediately: $2,

Look here to see what the IRS wants you to do.

As we notified you before, our records show you have unpaid taxes for the tax year ending December 31, 2010 (Form 1040). If you don't call us immediately or pay the amount due by October 6, 2011, we may seize ("levy") any state tax refund to which you're entitled and apply it to the $2, you owe.

If you still have an outstanding balance after we seize any state tax refund, we may take possession of your other property or your rights to property

Billing Summary

Amount you owed	$2,
Failure-to-pay penalty	
Interest charges	
Amount due immediately	**$2,2**

If you delay, notice how things may get difficult for you.

What you need to do immediately

Pay immediately

- Send us the amount due of $2, or we may seize ("levy") your state tax refund on or after October 6, 2011.

Continued on back.

IRS

Notice	CP504
Notice date	
Social Security number	

- Make your check or money order payable to the United States Treasury.
- Write your Social Security number (526-55-0317), the tax year (2010), and the form number (1040) on your payment and any correspondence.

Payment

INTERNAL REVENUE SERVICE
FRESNO, CA 93888-0025

Amount due immediately $2,

EXAMPLE OF A TYPICAL IRS NOTICE

CHAPTER FOUR

IT'S MY TAXPREPARER'S FAULT!

Who can prepare my tax return?

Anyone at all can prepare a tax return for you. Regardless of whether the preparer is very skilled or has no skill whatsoever, there are no limitations on who prepares your tax return. On the other hand, *you* have to sign the return, and *you are responsible for its contents*. Given the complicated nature of taxes, most returns are prepared by either a paid tax preparer or are self-prepared using software.

– Anyone you pay to prepare your tax return must be registered

If you pay someone to prepare your taxes, some restrictions apply. Any person that you pay to prepare your tax return must have a Preparer Tax ID Number (PTIN). A PTIN must be obtained by all tax preparers who are compensated for preparing or assisting in the preparation of all, or substantially all, of any U.S. federal tax return or claim for refund. Anyone who prepares a tax return for you must enter on the tax form their PTIN number. This is a way for the IRS to identify the person that assisted you with your tax return. With a PTIN, a tax preparer may refer to himself as a "Registered Tax Preparer".

What is a "Registered Tax Return Preparer?"

Tax preparation services prepare more than 50% of all tax returns filed in the U.S. annually. Because of the complexity of the tax code, these services are often the "go to" source for individual taxpayers. Many of these companies provide outstanding service and support. Some are well known retail chains and others are small local businesses that have been preparing neighborhood returns for generations. These companies hire tax preparers who do the actual preparation of your tax return.

Tax preparers can be very skilled persons who have years of experience, take continuing education classes and are thoughtful and diligent. Then there are the "others". Almost anyone can obtain a PTIN by paying an IRS fee of less than $70. Said another way, just because your tax preparer has a PTIN number, does not mean that he or she is knowledgeable or even competent. Anyone with a PTIN can buy a pretty certificate for his or her wall from a vendor. The certificates I have seen look official and look a lot like a diploma. These certificates are not issued by the IRS.

In fairness, the PTIN system is an effort by the IRS to improve the quality of tax returns. Paid tax preparers, like you might find in the chain retail tax preparation business, receive minimum training and often have a minimum amount of experience. Typically the retail tax preparation business is seasonal, meaning the stores are open only for the tax season from about January 15 through April 15. Tax preparers are hired just for the season and frequently have no prior experience. For most, all of their training is done in the store, for about 2 nights a week, for 8-12 weeks.

Studies have recommended that standards be set before someone can be paid to prepare your tax return. By requiring preparers to register and obtain a PTIN number, the IRS sought to provide some oversight and create a base for future regulation of the tax preparation industry.

The IRS's plan was to introduce continuing education and testing for each registered tax preparer. It was thought that this would improve the quality of tax returns and thereby reduce the error rate. The tax industry has fought back. Although PTIN registration is still required, the regulatory aspect may be in doubt. A recent appeals court decision has held that the IRS does not have the authority to regulate tax preparers or make them pass an exam. Congress could pass legislation to require certain standards for tax preparers, but has not done so yet.

My Tax Preparer Screwed up My Return!

Unfortunately, mistakes and errors are made by tax preparers, even those using sophisticated software. The error usually occurs because the tax preparer lacked knowledge, adequate training or experience. To be fair, many errors are the fault of the taxpayer, not the preparer. This is because the customer did not fully answer questions about relationships, dependencies or earnings during their tax interview with the preparer.

– The majority of tax payers are honest and errors are unintentional

Most taxpayers are honest. A misleading answer is unintentional and occurs by reason of mistake or misunderstanding. A skilled tax preparer is aware that clients do not understand tax terminology and will ask additional questions or simplify questions to help the client. The largest error rate occurs in the area of self-employed individuals, earned income credit, claiming dependents and child tax credits.

Recovering Damages from the Tax Preparer

Let's assume that your tax preparer is entirely responsible for a mistake in your tax return. How much liability does the preparer have for his or her mistake? Generally, you can recover from the tax preparer for the damages caused by his or her negligence. Damages may include interest, penalties, and incidental damages.

Interest

Interest that is incurred because of additional tax that results from the preparer's negligence may be a compensable recovery. Note, however, that at least one court has held that since you have had the use of the money the tax preparer should not be responsible for the interest that accrued.

Penalties

Penalties may also be recoverable. When a tax return is incorrectly prepared or filed, there may be penalties for late filing, late paying, or, more seriously, for intentional disregard of the rules and regulations. If at fault, a paid tax preparer should willingly pay these penalties.

Incidental Damages

There may also be incidental damages that you can recover. Incidental damages are things like lost investment opportunities because of the tax deficiency arising from a preparer's mistake.

Taxes

Unfortunately, you cannot recover the taxes that you would have paid, had the return been correctly prepared. Why? The reason is that you would have owed the tax anyway. Just because your tax preparer made a mistake that underreported your income, or overstated your deductions, the correct amount of tax was still due.

Case Study

Jon and Kyla have their taxes prepared by B&B Tax Service. They are married and have one child together (Bill) and Kyla has one child by a prior relationship (Sue). Kyla lost her job and did not work for the entire year. On their tax return, they claim the child tax credit for both children, even though Kyla lives with her father all year. Because they claimed a credit that they were not entitled to claim, their refund was $1000 larger than it should have been.

The IRS has sent them a notice to pay back the excess refund. If the tax preparer knew or should have known that they did not meet the support or relationship tests, then B&B Tax Service is responsible for the interest and penalty. B&B is not responsible for the larger tax that would have been owed if the return had been correctly prepared.

You are Responsible for Your Tax Return

You are responsible for your tax return even if someone else prepares your return for you. It seems paradoxical; you hire a tax person because they have superior knowledge and education about taxes, but you are just as responsible for the return as if you had prepared it by yourself.

– Even if you hire a tax preparer, you are still responsible for a correctly prepared and timely filed tax return. Ask questions.

For this reason, you must be engaged in the tax return process. Ask questions. Give full and complete answers when the preparer inquires about deductions, family relationships, job expenses and the like. You don't have to understand taxes, but you do know the basic information about you. It is your job to communicate it to the tax preparer.

If something does not sound right, or seems too good to be true, ask for an explanation. If you are uncomfortable, you can always tell the preparer to put your return on hold. You can leave the preparer's office and call the IRS to ask a question, or even go to a different tax office.

Abusive Tax Preparers

The IRS advises caution in hiring your tax preparer and suggests that you look at free information on the IRS web site before hiring a preparer (www.irs.gov). The IRS also advises that it can help many taxpayers prepare their own returns without the assistance of a paid preparer.

I am skeptical that the IRS really can help. As mentioned earlier, the IRS has cut 3,300 customer assistance employees from its payroll. Customer service was never all that great, even before the staffing cuts.

The IRS does offer good advice about things that you should consider when you hire a tax return preparer. Below are the main points:

- Be wary of tax return preparers who claim they can obtain larger refunds than others.
- Avoid tax return preparers who base their fee on a percentage of the refund (its illegal).
- Use a reputable tax professional who furnishes his PTIN.
- The preparer must sign the return and the PTIN must also be entered on the return.
- Reputable preparers will request to see your records and receipts.
- Never sign a blank tax return.
- Review the entire return before signing.
- Obtain a copy of your tax return from the preparer.

- Check the person's credentials. Only attorneys, CPAs and enrolled agents can represent taxpayers before the IRS in all matters including audits, collection and appeals.

If you have been scammed by a tax preparer or you believe there have been unethical practices, you can make a complaint to the IRS. Examples of illegal or unethical practices include:

- Failing to sign a tax return they prepare or to use a PTIN number
- Failing to provide a customer copy of their return
- Preparing a tax return using the customer's last pay stub (must use a W-2)
- Creating false exemptions or dependents
- Altering documents
- Embezzling a client's funds
- Falsely claiming to be a certified public accountant or enrolled agent

To file a complaint, use IRS form 14157, downloadable from the IRS web site at www.irs.gov. The instructions for completing the form are with the form. Mail your completed complaint to the Return Preparer Office. The mailing address is included with the download.

CHAPTER FIVE

THE COLLECTION PROCESS

Overview

The mission of the Internal Revenue Service is to administer the tax laws efficiently, fairly and with the least amount of burden to the taxpayer. It's widely publicized the IRS doesn't always meet this goal. The IRS can be very heavy-handed, and, for most taxpayers the actions are incomprehensible. The purpose of this chapter is to give you some insight into how the IRS processes collections.

– The IRS can be very heavy-handed in collecting tax, know your rights

Tax Reform

The IRS is the largest collection agency in the world. It collects all the revenue for the United States anywhere in the world. Because of the heavy-handed approach of the IRS in collecting, Congress became involved in an effort to make the playing field more level and pass the 1998 IRS Restructuring and Reform Act. This restructuring also included a Taxpayer Bill of Rights.

The purpose of the 1998 Reform Act was to make customer service and efficient claim handling the top goals of the IRS. In fact, the IRS did change, sometimes for the better; sometimes the changes were merely bureaucratic and more political than substantive.

Today, it is my opinion the IRS is slipping back to a more aggressive pre-1998 posture. In 2012, the taxpayer Advocate reported to Congress that because of an expanding workload and declining funding, the IRS is not meeting its own goals.

> "This is causing the IRS to resort to shortcuts that undermine fundamental taxpayer rights and harm taxpayers-and at the same time reduces the IRS' ability to deliver on its core mission of raising revenue," - Nina Olson, Tax Payer Advocate.

Add to that the fact that Congress has decreased IRS funding for each of the past two years. The situation is also made worse because the IRS is now tasked with administering the Affordable Care Act (Obama Care). The IRS lost 10,000 employees between 2010 and 2013 according to the trade publication "Accounting Today". In 2013 the IRS lost an additional 3,300 employees in tax payer assistance programs alone. Bad news if you expect help from the IRS.

Automated Collection System

The first level of contact that you are likely to have is the IRS' Automated Collection System (ACS). The system stores basic information about every taxpayer. When you file a tax return, it is scanned, and information from the return is posted to IRS computers.

If you owe money, a series of collection letters will be automatically generated and sent to you by mail. Each collection letter will ask for payment and will give you a telephone number to call. Unfortunately, if you telephone, the hold times are notoriously long. Recently it has been reported that a rising number of calls are never answered.

When your call is answered, it will be routed to a customer service center where a representative will identify herself and give you her IRS employee identification number. You will then be asked for your information. At that point, the representative will pull up your file from the IRS computer system, and you can begin your conversation about your concern or issue.

Anything You Say…

Be aware that the primary purpose of the call center is to collect money from you. Therefore, any information that you give the representative will be recorded and used to collect back taxes. It has been the experience of many people that the IRS representative will not be able to give you a full explanation. Rather, he or she will simply read what's in your tax transcript, but often cannot explain the entry in the transcript. It does no good to argue with the IRS representative.

– Any information you give the IRS will be entered into the collection system. Don't lie, but do be careful about what you say.

Currently, customer service at the IRS is so bad that, at the slightest indication of argument or "attitude", the IRS representative will transfer you to another telephone queue. You will be on hold and when (or if) you get through to a live person; you will have to start again, repeating the same information that you gave the first representative. It is common for the representative to pass you on to a collector who has limited authority to make payment arrangements.

Automated Dialer

Like any collection agency, the IRS will telephone you. The ACS system includes an automated dialer. An IRS employee may call you on your home phone, your work phone or even your cell phone. The ACS system automatically records the number of attempts there were made to telephone you and the result of each call.

Notices and Letters

I have already mentioned the automatic generation of notices and letters. Normally, a taxpayer will receive a series of four (4) notices. The first notice will be mild. It is a "request for payment" and is required by law. This notice informs the taxpayer that a tax is due, states the amount of tax and any interest and penalties apply. The notice also demands payment within 10 to 21 days.

The next correspondence will be an "Urgent, Immediate action is required" notice which will be sent approximately 5 weeks after the first notice. Thereafter, also at approximately 5 week intervals, you will receive further notices.

– Pay attention to a CP 504 Notice because it has legal significance

The fourth notice is the CP 504 Notice. This is a serious notice to which you need to pay attention. It is intended to give you legal notice that the IRS will levy against any state tax refund. In addition, the IRS will begin to search for assets on which a levy can be placed, as, for example, your wages. The IRS may record a tax lien in the County in which you reside which will encumber all real property that you may own. An example of the CP 504 Notice is shown in the chapter "Your IRS Notice or Letter".

CHAPTER SIX

WHO, ME?

At this point, you may think the IRS must have made a mistake. If so, you should telephone the IRS. Plan to set aside at least an hour, as you will be "on hold" for time that frequently exceeds 30 minutes. You will be routed to an IRS representative (discussed earlier in this chapter), and this may not be a satisfactory experience for you. The IRS representative is interested in collections, not solutions. Even so, you should at least make an effort to telephone. You will gain information and insight. You will be asked to give financial information about where you work and your bank accounts. Like any good collector, the IRS employee will want you to make a promise to pay or a promise to send financial information to the IRS. If you make a promise, that your promise will be noted in the IRS system.

— If you make a payment promise it will be noted in the IRS system

If there is a mistake in your tax return or some other issue, such as incorrect W-2 statements, you will not be able to resolve the issue on the telephone. As previously mentioned, the telephone representative is there to collect money, extract a promise of payment or gather information about you. Any real correction of a mistake will need to be done by letter and backed up by written explanation and documentation.

How Much Time Do I Have?

You really don't have much time. The IRS will wait 30 - 45 days after which it takes enforcement actions that are more serious than mere notices. If you don't pay or make arrangements to pay, the IRS has a toolkit of options. Don't be fooled into thinking that the IRS cannot locate your job or assets. Nearly every transaction involving wages, investments, retirement accounts buying or selling real property or the ownership in a business or partnership, leaves a paper trail. Modernly, nearly every payment to an employee, independent contractor or vendor must be summarized and electronically transmitted to the IRS at year-end. Many states have automated sharing of information with the IRS.

Don't Depend on Receiving Every Notice

The IRS has some discretion in deciding whether to send you all notices. Factors that will be considered are whether or not you are a "repeater" having had previous collection actions, or have previous years of unfiled tax returns. If the IRS has reason to believe that you have assets that you intend to dispose of or that you will attempt to hide, the collection process can be accelerated dramatically.

If the taxpayer has a history of delinquency or already owes unpaid taxes, he or she will likely receive only a few notices. If the tax bill is large, enforcement action may be moved up, and fewer notices will be sent.

Special Note for Business Owners

If there are unpaid employment taxes, the IRS becomes very aggressive, very quickly. You should expect a personal visit by a Revenue Officer. This is because payroll taxes include the withholding from employee's checks. Employee withholdings are considered trust fund monies which you pay over to the IRS, but in which you have no rights. If only income taxes are involved, the IRS will likely still send fewer notices, omitting the second and third notices previously mentioned.

Last Chance Notice

If you do not respond by paying the taxes due, or setting up a payment program the IRS will prepare to take legal action. You will receive an IRS letter, often form letter LTR 11 or letter 1058, "FINAL NOTICE-NOTICE OF INTENT TO LEVY AND NOTICE OF YOUR RIGHT TO A HEARING-PLEASE RESPOND IMMEDIATELY".

You may also receive Letter 3172 "NOTICE OF FEDERAL TAX LIEN FILING AND YOU'RE RIGHT TO A HEARING UNDER IRC 6320". These letters are telling you that the Service intends to levy your wages or bank accounts, and it will perhaps seize assets. Enforcement action can occur in as soon as 30 days. Examples of assets that may be seized include:

- Wages, real estate commissions and other income
- Bank accounts
- Business assets
- Personal assets (including your car and home)
- Social Security benefits

Each Tax Year is Separately Assessed

Sometimes it may appear that the IRS is sending you multiple notices of the same kind. When this happens, you should look closely at the year or years for which the notice applies. This will be usually in the middle of the page or in the upper right corner of the CP notice. Each tax year is assessed separately. When you have the attention of the IRS, they may send you a notice for one tax year and then because of the computerized system they will send you another notice for a different year for which a tax return or taxes are due.

Case Study – Multiple Notices

Matt and Lizbeth moved from St. Louis to Los Angeles 5 years ago in 2007. When then got to L.A., they had to find a place to live, get new jobs and had all of the usual expenses that happen when people move. Because they were short on money, they did not file a tax return for 2007. Nothing happened, so they thought they could skip filing a return for the next year. In 2009, they had a temporary separation and neither one of them filed a return for that year. They reconciled in the following year. In June 2013, the IRS started sending notices for 2007. Later in the same month, they started receiving more notices.

Both Matt and Lizbeth thought these were repeat mailings of the first notices they received, because they looked exactly like the first set of notices. In reality, the IRS was only catching up, sending a different set of notices for each year of non-filing. Because of their inattention, their bank accounts and Matt's wages were both levied.

Unfortunately, without their savings as a buffer, they could not recover from being a month behind on all their bills and suffered a repossession of Matt's car. All of this could have avoided if they had realized that multiple years were involved and they had acted earlier to obtain help with their tax problem. Later they obtained the help of a tax attorney who was able to stop the wage levy.

IRS Gathers Information about You

It is at this point that the IRS will actively begin looking for assets. The IRS may contact your employer, contact your neighbors or credit sources and make inquiries about your employment, income and your assets. Your account may also be referred to a Revenue Officer in your local area. The Revenue Officer may make in person visits. The Revenue Officer may contact you at your home or place of work or invite you to the local IRS office for an "interview".

– Obtain representation for any interview. An innocent remark may result in additional years coming under investigation

Remember that anything you say to the IRS can and will be held against you. You should be represented because even an innocent remark can result in additional tax years coming under investigation. In almost every instance, you should say to the revenue officer that you are willing to cooperate, but you need to speak with your attorney first. Often, a person is startled when a knock at the door is a Revenue Officer on your doorstep. Of course you want cooperate, that goes without saying. But, you do not want to make inadvertent admissions or statements that will adversely affect your case with the IRS.

Criminal Investigations

Some tax violations are criminal. The IRS Criminal Investigation Division (CID) investigates cases that may involve tax evasion or tax fraud. Cases are referred to CID by IRS Revenue Officers or other agencies. If warranted, CID also refers the case to other parts of the IRS. CID investigations often run parallel to civil tax investigations. In other words, the information obtained by you Revenue Officer will be shared with criminal investigations Special Agents and vice versa.

A criminal tax case involves a willful violation of law. "Willful violation" is a special term of legal art. The difference between a mere civil prosecution and criminal prosecution can sometimes be a very fine line. Often the decision to prosecute criminally depends on policy considerations that may change from administration to administration. Examples of hot button issues for criminal investigation include abusive tax schemes, fraud, undisclosed income and offshore accounts.

Although it is useful to think that criminal investigations and prosecution results only from large dollar crimes, it is not always accurate. Of particular interest are cases where individuals engage in any pattern of conduct such as filing false tax returns using someone else's Social Security number; schemes intended to generate large refunds through falsely claiming dependents and similar such conduct.

Don't Be Talkative

If you are contacted by CID, the agents will identify themselves and show identification. Write down the names and identification numbers of both agents. Now is not the time to become nervous and talkative. Keep cool. It is especially important that you delay discussing anything with the CID Special Agents until you obtain the advice of an attorney. Many a case has been lost because a taxpayer made inadvertent statements under the stress and nervousness of the contact.

Case Study – Inadvertent Admissions

The best example of an inadvertent statement in a criminal case is in the movie "My Cousin Vinny". Ralph Macchio plays the part of Billy Gambini, who is arrested with his friend, after accidently taking a can of tuna from a convenience store. Later the store clerk is murdered, and Billy Gambini and his friend are arrested for the murder.

During interrogation, the sheriff accuses Billy of shooting and killing the clerk. Billy answers incredulously, "I shot the clerk? I shot the clerk?!" Later a transcript is read in court, but of course the incredulous tone does not come through when the witness reads the plain words from the transcript, "I shot the clerk". The statement was admitted into evidence as an admission of guilt for the murder.

Rule #1. Resist the temptation of trying to "clear things up" when talking to CID agents. Call your lawyer instead. Anything you say before you are represented can be an admission against your business or financial interests.

Rule #2. See Rule #1.

CHAPTER SEVEN

DO YOU OWE?

Are Income Taxes Legal?

A question that often comes up in conversation is whether or not it is legal for the IRS to collect income tax from U.S. citizens. It's probably best to get this issue out of the way up front. A tax protester is someone who refuses to pay a tax on constitutional or legal grounds by claiming that there is no authority for Congress to impose taxes on its own citizens.

Generally these arguments center on a claim that the Sixteenth Amendment was never properly ratified by the states and/or that being forced to file a tax return violates the Fifth Amendment right against self-incrimination. The courts have addressed this on a number of occasions. The simple fact is that there is no legal validity to these arguments. In fact, raising a "tax protester" argument can often be interpreted as a willful violation of tax law resulting in increased civil penalties and perhaps even criminal prosecution.

Practical Considerations

Some people are diehards. They will still insist that taxation under the present system is unconstitutional. Let me tell you why, in a practical sense, it doesn't matter. Your tax case is going to be about your taxes and not theoretical arguments. As a practical matter, to assert a constitutionality of taxation argument, you have to move your case through Tax Court through the Court of Appeals and up to the Supreme Court. This takes a lot of money, and is almost certainly a lot more money than you have at stake in paying your taxes. Further, the IRS and the lower courts are so disgusted with the tax protester arguments that you will not get any real consideration for your argument. Therefore you should look at this practically and frame your defense within the rules that are acknowledged to exist i.e. the Internal Revenue Code.

What's Income?

Gross income is "all income from whatever source derived". It includes income from services you perform, income derived from business, gains from dealing in property, rents, royalties, dividends, alimony (but not child support) … and six other categories. The short answer is that if you receive a benefit from a transaction or perform services for someone else, the value of the benefit or services is considered to be income to you.

On your tax return, you are required to self-report income. Generally speaking, income is either "Earned Income" or "Not Earned Income" which includes "passive income". There are some different nuances but for our purposes these two categories will encompass most of the income issues that you are likely to run into.

Earned income includes all taxable income and wages you get for working for someone who pays you or if you own your own business or farm. Earned income includes:

- Wages;
- Salaries;
- Tips;
- Other taxable employee pay, Union strike benefits; Long-term disability benefits (received prior to minimum retirement age);
- Net earnings from self-employment

Military Personnel

If you are in the military there are special rules that may apply to you, particularly with regard to combat pay. Be sure to ask your tax preparer about exclusions that may apply to you.

Unemployment Compensation

A note about unemployment income. Frequently people are confused about whether unemployment compensation is taxable. Supplemental unemployment benefits received from your company are considered "taxable wages". Unemployment compensation received from a state is taxable as "other income". Congress has contributed to this confusion because in a prior year a portion of unemployment compensation was excluded from taxation.

However, as of this writing and as is true in most years, unemployment compensation is considered taxable income. If you should find yourself in the unfortunate situation of being unemployed, be sure to have your state unemployment division withhold a portion of your unemployment compensation. This will save you from owing taxes at the end of the year; taxes that you won't be able to pay because you are unemployed.

Passive income/Not Earned Income

Other income that you receive may be taxable but still not be considered as earned income. Examples are interest income, dividends, retirement income, social security and alimony. Each of these types of income is subject to special rules and some have exclusions. These rules are too complex to be addressed in this book. What you do need to know is that each is handled differently on your tax return and many require reporting and schedules (think of these as attachments) to your income tax return.

How the IRS learns About Your Income

People are often surprised that the IRS is able to learn about their sources of income. Over the years, the laws regarding third-party reporting of all types of income have become stricter. As a result, the IRS gathers more and more information about taxpayers every year. In addition, the IRS's computers are becoming more sophisticated and are doing a much better job today of matching income to individuals than in the past.

The most familiar form is, of course, the W-2. This is a wage earner statement that reports earnings and withholdings of an employee. Employers are required to report these earnings to the Social Security Administration, which shares the information with the IRS.

Another type of earnings from work is an independent contractor or a vendor's form 1099-MISC. Anyone who has paid at least $600 in rents, services (including parts and materials), prizes or awards is required to issue a 1099-MISC. If you are self-employed, you will likely receive a separate 1099-MISC from each company to which you provided services during the year. Beware of unreported cash payments or "under the table" payments that may cause trouble for you later.

Case Study

Ron is a landscaper. He is very diligent in keeping books and records for his business and reports on his tax return his income from landscaping.

Ron also performs weekly lawn maintenance. His customers usually pay him for this work in cash. One of his customers is Geoff. In 2013 Geoff paid $100/mo. for lawn maintenance to Ron. At the end of the year, Geoff's accountant sees the payments and follows the law by preparing a 1099-MISC, sending a copy to both Ron and the IRS as required.

Ron is now under audit for the unreported income. During the audit, the IRS finds 20 other lawn maintenance customers each of whom has paid the various amounts to Ron, "under the table". Ron now has a sizable tax liability for $35,150 in unreported income. If the IRS determines this was a wilful and intentional evasion of tax law, he could also face criminal prosecution.

Third Party Payments to You

There are many different transactions that third party payers are required to report to the IRS. For example, a 1099-INT reports interest payments to you, and 1099-DIV reports dividend payments. Your unemployment compensation payment received from your state government is reported to the IRS and to you on form 1099-G. For gambling winnings you will receive form W2-G and the casino will also report the winnings to the IRS.

Disputed Income

If the IRS receives a report of income that you did not state on your tax return, it will send you a notice and will recalculate your tax liability using the additional income. It goes without saying that additional income will increase your taxable income and will result in a balance due. The letter you receive will likely be a CP 2000 notice.

Omitted income letters can be a little tricky. The IRS will usually print a grid or table on the 2nd or 3rd page of the notice that will inform you of the source of the additional income and the increase of decrease for each item (there may be more than one W-2 or 1099).

Usually you have to know something about how the income is reported on an actual tax return, because the IRS does not always give a line number to use as a reference. Each line of a tax return form has a separate line number. If the line number is stated in the letter, it is much easier to see what the IRS changed. Sometimes a line number reference is not included with the IRS letter and you will have to figure out on your own where the difference occurs.

I Did Not Receive A W-2 (Or 1099-MISC)

Anyone who pays a contractor or vendor more than $600 for services is required to send that person a 1099-MISC. In the case of wages, the employer must provide the employee a W-2. In both cases, the payor is also required to send an electronic copy to the IRS (1099-MISC) or to Social Security Administration. Employers report employee wages to the SSA on a SSA copy of your W-2. SSA transmits the payroll information to the IRS. Modernly, actual forms are not used, as the data is transmitted electronically, vastly reducing the time for the IRS to match wages to your tax return.

– Not receiving a wage or income statement is not a legal excuse for not filing a tax return

File Your Return

Keep in mind that just because you did not receive the W-2 or 1099 does not mean that you didn't receive the income. By law, you are obligated to report the income regardless of whether you receive the appropriate informational form from your employer or payor. You are required make a good faith estimate of wages or income and report it on your income tax return. You can use bank records showing deposits, log books, work schedules, job report sheets and anything else that in logic and reason is a reasonable means to estimation.

– If you did not receive a W-2 or 1099, estimate your income

Corrected W-2 or 1099-MISC

If you actually were not paid the amount shown on the form (or you did receive income but the amount shown is not correct) you can dispute it. You can try to telephone the number on the letter. However the IRS employee on the other end of the line does not have the authority to change anything. The usual response is to either tell you to write the IRS. Sometimes you will be mailed an appropriate form to fill out and attach to your letter. Sometimes you will get another CP 2000 notice in the mail, and nothing more.

To dispute a W-2 or 1099, you should first telephone the payor. If the payor agrees with you, the payor should issue you a corrected informational form. In the case of wages, the form would be a W-2C. Send the corrected copy to the IRS Service Center with your tax return. If you already filed based on a good faith estimate, you must file an amended return using the figures on the correct copy.

Report a Missing or Incorrect Wage or Earnings Statement (W-2 or 1099-R)

If the payor will not cooperate, you still have a remedy. If the W-2 or 1099-R is incorrect, submit IRS Form 4852. This is a multi-purpose form for claiming that income was reported to you was incorrect. You can obtain the form mentioned below from the IRS web site. Complete it and mail it to the IRS address on your CP 2000 notice. Write a brief letter explaining the problem and staple it to the IRS form. When received, the IRS will send a letter to your employer or payor inquiring about your complaint and advising the payor of their responsibilities to provide a correct W-2 or 1099.

Report a Missing or Incorrect 1099-MISC

If you received a 1099-MISC that is incorrect, enter the correct amount on your tax return and prepare a written explanation that you will attach to your tax return when you file. Some will advise you to call the IRS to report the problem. In my experience this is not useful. Instead, wait for the IRS to contact you about the difference between what you reported and what was reported on the 1099-MISC. Be ready to reply to the IRS with another copy of your explanation plus any documentation that supports the amount you reported on your tax return.

If the employer still claims that the W-2 or 1099 is correct you can win, but it does become harder to do. You will have to "prove" that you did not receive the income. Proving a negative can be difficult because you need some form of documentation.

– Proving a negative is difficult, but you can provide evidence on non-receipt of payment through the absence of deposits in bank records or business or accounting records regularly kept

You will have to think about what kind of documents might tend to show earnings. For example if you worked as a server and tip income is overstated, provide a copy of your tips book with dated entries for your tip outs to front of house and back of house staff. If you are truck driver, use your log books to show your mileage or duty hours and deliveries. There is almost always some alternative way for you to make a reasonable estimate of income that you actually received.

– The payor must maintain books and records to show that you were in fact paid the amount claimed

The IRS will also make inquiry of the payor. Businesses are required to maintain regularly maintained books and accounting records. If the business claims they made a payment to you that you did not receive, the business should be able to back up the claim with a cancelled check or evidence of an electronic transfer. If the payment was in cash, the business should have your signature on a receipt for the cash payment.

CHAPTER EIGHT

THE IRS DISALLOWED MY DEDUCTION OR CREDIT

Now what?

The leading cause for adjustments of returns by the IRS (meaning you will owe more taxes) is because a deduction or credit you took on your tax return was disallowed. "Disallowed" simply means that the IRS thinks the deduction was overstated or that the credit was one that you should not have taken, thereby increasing your taxable income.

As with every other aspect of the Internal Revenue Code, the rules for proper allowance of deductions and credits are complicated and are highly political. In fact, much of the tax code deals with deductions and credits, the so-called "loopholes". Note that these "loopholes" are publicized as applying only to the rich. Actually, that's not exactly true. A large number of credits and deductions are available to individual taxpayers. In the limited space available in this book, it is not possible to explain every deduction or credit. We do want to describe for you the common types of problems that we see in our practice that affect average taxpayers. In the following paragraphs are some of the issues that come up frequently.

Please note that this book is not intended to be a primer on how to prepare taxes. The goal is to help you understand the "where and why" of a proposed IRS adjustment and give you a place to start in attacking the IRS's proposed adjustment before it becomes an assessment of tax.

Dependent Exemptions

You may take an exemption for yourself, your spouse and any dependents. An exemption reduces your taxable income. Exemptions are important because the amount of the exemption is treated as if you never received that amount as income. Said another way, if you had a choice between an exemption and a deduction, you would always be better off with choosing an exemption.

The hot action in the IRS's examination of tax returns is in the claiming of exemptions to which a taxpayer is not entitled. A dependent exemption is the gateway that opens the door to being able to claim certain credits. This issue is often hotly contested between divorced couples because it makes a real difference in the tax that you pay or the refund to which you are entitled. It is also ripe for tax fraud, because it is relatively easy to claim a dependent that does not exist using a stolen social security number.

You may claim a person or your child as a dependent if certain tests are met. Generally these tests center on support and the relationship of the person to you. Things become more complex if the child has not lived with you for more than half the year, in divorce situations where one spouse claims child as a dependent or where another relative has claimed a person or child as a dependent. For example a grandparent may be providing both housing and support and therefore may be able to claim the grandchild as a dependent.

When the IRS disallows a dependent it is usually because of questions about support or the relationship of the child to you. You may have to submit evidence that you are the person responsible for the custody of the child and that you have provided more than one half of the child's support for the year.

– Use custody orders or school records to show you that the child lived with you for most of the year

To respond to a disallowed credit, you will need to reply to the IRS letter and provide documentation about the specific item or issue that the IRS has questioned. To show that the child lived with you, provide a copy of a custody order from a court. If you don't have a custody order, then provide a school record showing the child's enrollment with your home address or something similar. To show support, you need state in your reply that you provided more than ½ of the child's support for the year. You may need to provide the IRS with a copy of a utility bill, mortgage or rent statement, in your name and with your address to support your claim.

Child Tax Credits

A credit of up to $1000 per child may be allowed if the child is a "qualifying child". This is a term of art used by the IRS but basically means that the child must be under the age of 17, have a familial relationship and meet the dependent and support test. Sometimes citizenship or residency can be an issue. The IRS may state in a notice or letter the specific test about which it is inquiring. More often, you will receive a form letter with laundry list. Take your time and respond to each item, one by one.

Business Deductions

Whether you're self-employed, running a small business from your home or have a corporation with separate offices, you have business expenses. Disallowed business expenses commonly result from the amount claimed, the nature of the claimed expense or inadequate documentation.

The general rule is that to be a deductible business expense it must be both "ordinary and necessary" for the business activity. An expense is an ordinary expense if it is one that is common and accepted in your trade or business. There is no clear black and white rule about what is "common and accepted".

– IRS auditors have wide discretion to disallow a deduction. Explain to the agent why the expense is necessary for your business activities

Every auditor has discretion to allow or disallow a deduction based on his or her interpretation. In deducting business expenses use common sense. Occasionally, we have to be very patient with the IRS employee examining your return to explain a questioned business deduction. It seems that "common sense" is really not very common at all in the government. Explain to the agent why the expense is necessary for your business activities.

Sometimes business owners mix personal expenses with business expenses. For example, one of the first questions the IRS may ask you is "Does the business pay for your truck?" If the answer is yes, then you will need to show how much of the truck usage is for your personal use (such as driving to and from the office) and how much is used on business related activities. To the extent that the truck is used for personal use, you will have to report that as income to you. The business will deduct the difference as wages paid to you.

Case study – Business Use vs. Personal Use

Jonas owns a painting business. His company bought a truck that Jonas uses to drive back and forth from his home to his office. He also uses the truck on the weekends for running around town. He uses the truck to check on jobs and call on customers. Assuming that the monthly payment on the truck is $300 (($3600/yr.) and his personal mileage is 50% of the total, the company can only deduct ½ of the truck payment and must report the other ½ ($1800) as income paid to Jonas.

The personal versus business use question comes up in other ways. For example, if you borrow money and use 70% of the loan for business and 30% for a family vacation, then only 70% of the interest is deductible as an expense to the business. The remaining interest is personal interest and is not deductible.

Inadequately Documented Expenses

Frequently business expenses are disallowed because the taxpayer did not provide sufficient documentation to prove that the expense was incurred. This is a "substantiation" issue. If the original documents, such as receipts no longer exist, you might be able to substantiate the expense using other records such as cancelled checks, credit card statements or by asking your supplier for copies of invoices that you paid.

CHAPTER NINE

AUDITS

According to the IRS, an audit is a review/examination of an organization's or individual's accounts and financial information to ensure information is being reported correct, according to the tax laws, to verify the amount of tax reported is correct.

When we speak of audits we often have a mental picture of a taxpayer in an interrogation room sweatbox with an IRS agent standing over him, pencil in hand, adding up new tax. Fortunately for taxpayers, the IRS is short staffed. It has become more selective about the returns it audits, doing fewer but expecting better results from each. An audit will end with either a "no change" recommendation by the auditor or a proposed adjustment. Adjustments recommendations are made in about 80% of all audits.

Notwithstanding that fact, the IRS is examines more returns as its computer matching technology improves. The IRS has many ways to check return information, other than by a formal audit. For example, a letter or notice from the IRS asking for additional information is a form of audit. A large number of adjustments are made by the IRS's automated under reporting program or the non-filer program. We have discussed elsewhere in this book notices, assessments and penalties.

Some audits are purely random. More often there is something about the tax return, or information supplied by third parties, that result in your return being flagged for audit. For readers of this book, the two main areas are underreporting and underpayment of tax. The IRS uses a computer scoring system initially to select returns. Some of the items that are scored are:

- The comparative size of the item in relation to other items on the return
- The context in which the item is stated
- The relationship of the item to other items on the return
- Any evidence of intent to mislead

An audit is done in one of three ways: correspondence examinations, field examinations or office audits. Correspondence examinations are the most common as they are the most cost effective. These often arrive on your doorstep as a letter or notice that requests additional information.

Field Examinations are conducted by revenue officers located in an IRS field office. It may involve a detailed examination of books and records at your home or place of business. The IRS may issue summons to compel third parties to produce documents. Also, agents may interview your neighbors, customers or business associates to find out more about you. There is a risk that the field examination may be opened to include other tax years. Field examinations can be complex and may span more than a single issue and may require multiple visits by the revenue officer.

The office audit is conducted at the IRS local office. It might fairly be said that office audits fall in the middle, in terms of complexity, between correspondence and field audits. Frequent office audit issues involve questioned income, head of household filing status, dependent exemptions, credits and deductions taken by self-employed persons or small businesses.

Taxpayer Rights during Audit

During the audit, you have rights. The revenue agent will not always tell you about your rights. Intimidation is not an official IRS policy, but the nature of an audit gives the auditor great powers of intimidation. A stern look, a well timed "hmm…" after looking at a receipt, or body language; all can used effectively to cause you discomfort. The IRS can contact third parties which may disrupt your personal and business relationships. Knowing your rights will help you keep your balance and composure. These rights include:

- A written request for specific documents needed
- A right to professional and courteous treatment by IRS employees
- A right to privacy and confidentiality in tax matters
- A right to know why the IRS is asking for information
- A right to record any interview
- A right to representation
- A right to appeal disagreed tax positions
- Attorney-Client privilege

No Shoe Box Records, Please!

Some people keep all of their receipts in a shoe box or shopping bag. (Literally. I have had clients bring in a paper bag full of receipts). With today's software, it is amazingly easy to keep your receipts organized. Most people enter them into QuickBooks™, and there are a host of new web based "cloud" applications, one example of which is

Freshbooks™. You may not need that much software power. Spreadsheet programs are widely available; some are free, such as Google Docs™ or OpenOffice™. For keeping track of your income and expenses, they are very easy to learn and use.

It is not enough just to enter a date, memo and amount in software. You will need to keep a copy of the actual receipt. This is a very basic step that many people skip. You have to discipline yourself to keep your receipts. Receipts are akin to the famous lost sock. Receipts hide in the bottom of your briefcase, in a pocket of a purse and under car seats. Dig them out, they are valuable.

– Keep receipts organized

Here is a simple and foolproof way to stay organized. Take an ordinary business envelope, and write the month on the outside of the envelope. Put the paper receipts for the month in that envelope. Better yet, go paperless. Buy an inexpensive scanner and scan all of your receipts. Now you are always ready with receipts for an IRS audit, or for other things that come up, like making a warranty claim on a defective product.

In-Person Interviews with Revenue Officer

Recently I was asked by a person who was about to go to an audit interview if it was "Ok" to hand the Revenue Officer his box of receipts. The answer is an unequivocal "No!"

– Under the Taxpayer Bill of Rights, you do not have to appear in person if you are represented

This person was going to represent himself at the audit interview, something that I never recommend. Remember this was to be an "in person" interview, not a review by telephone or mail. The assignment of a person meant that the IRS was already suspicious and it was willing to use an expensive resource to eyeball his books and records. The IRS is spread thin and does not commit field personnel without good reason. It would have been very easy for a nervous taxpayer to misunderstand the significance of a question asked by the Revenue Officer, and to make inadvertent admissions. Part of the Taxpayer Bill of Rights is a provision allowing an attorney to appear in the place of the taxpayer. In other words, a person who had representation would not have to appear in person at the interview.

Whether represented or not, never give all of your receipts to the agent. If you do, the agent may see something else of interest, which may lead to another audit item, or may even lead to opening audits on additional tax years. I recommend having all of your receipts entered onto a spreadsheet. If the agent asks about a particular deduction, have your receipts organized so that you can reach into an envelope pull out that particular receipt. Never volunteer anything. Your job is not to help the IRS find problems with your tax returns.

Concluding the Audit

A field audit or office audit will conclude with an exit interview with the IRS agent. An audit can be concluded in one of three ways: "No Change", "Agreed" or "Disagreed". An "agreed" audit is one in which you agree with the auditor's findings, and you agree to the proposed change. You will be asked to sign the auditor's examination report.

A "disagreed" audit is what the name implies; you do not agree with the IRS after the audit. You can disagree with some or all of the issues and findings. On disagreement, the IRS will issue a form letter, known as a "30 day letter". The name derives from the limitation period; you have only 30 days to take action. The letter will be accompanied by the Revenue Officer's Report which explains the agent's findings.

Your options after receiving a 30 day letter are to:

- Pay the proposed tax
- Appeal the audit
- Wait for a Notice of Deficiency

Paying the proposed tax stated in the letter settles the matter. If you question the manner or method of the audit examination, you may request to meet with an IRS manager. It may be possible to reach some middle ground and settle your case at this time. After receiving the 30 Day Letter, you may make a Deficiency Appeal to the IRS Appeals Office (See the chapter on Appeals).

A Notice of Deficiency is a letter that gives you notice of tax due. It is the government's legal notice that it has made a determination and that it intends to immediately assess and collect the tax. The letter allows you to contest the determination in Tax Court. You only have 90 days from the date of the notice to file a Tax Court Petition. This time limit is strictly enforced. Both your petition and the (currently $60) filing fee must be timely received at the court. The court cannot extend the time, and it does not have jurisdiction to hear your case if you miss the filing deadline.

⇨ See the chapter "Take the IRS to Court"

CHAPTER TEN

UNFILED RETURNS

The Internal Revenue Code imposes a variety of deadlines for both filing a tax return and paying the tax. The deadlines are not complicated. For most individuals, their tax return is due on April 15 of every year. If they filed for an automatic extension then the return is due on October 15. If the date falls on a weekend or holiday, then the next business day is when the return is due.

People don't file a return for a variety of reasons. Sometimes they think they are not required to file and other times it's a matter of procrastination or an inability to pay any tax. Their thinking is: "If I can't pay the tax, then I should not file because I don't want the IRS to send me a bill."

– Taxes are due and payable on the date the return is due, even if you obtained an extension to file or did not file a return

File a Return Even If You Cannot Pay

Not filing a return because you will get a tax bill is a really terrible strategy. The filing of the tax return and the paying of the tax are completely separate. Even if you can't pay, you should still file a tax return. There mere fact of failing to file can be a misdemeanor that can be punishable by jail or by fine and more commonly, there are civil penalties for failing to file a required return.

Can You Hide-Out?

There was, perhaps, a time when a person who did not file could slip under the radar and not caught by the IRS for years. As they say, "times, they are changing." And today disappearing is almost impossible. The IRS does computer matching of social security numbers with tax reporting forms like W-2s and 1099s. Therefore, the IRS will always know where you were working at the end of the year.

In some respects, failing to file a tax return is treated by the IRS more seriously than being delinquent on the tax bill itself. This is because the IRS believes that people who do not file are at risk for evading taxes or being repeat offenders. The IRS will carefully scrutinize non-filers for indications of fraud.

In addition to the civil penalties for failing to file, there is the real possibility of wage garnishment, bank levies and tax liens. A tax lien will negatively affect your credit and could prevent you from selling or buying real property without first paying a lien in full.

Substitute for Return prepared by IRS

If your returns remain unfiled after the IRS has requested you to file, the IRS will refer your case for an Automated Substitute for Return or to the Examination Division for preparation of a return by the Service. When the IRS does this, it is for the convenience of the government. It does not satisfy that requirement that *you* file a return.

When the IRS does prepare these returns, the amount of tax due is almost always higher than what the taxpayer would have owed if he had filed for himself. This is because the IRS prepares the substitute return solely based on income reported to it or estimated by the IRS. You filing status is automatically assigned as either single or married filing separately; you don't get the benefit of dependent deductions, other deductions or credits that you may be entitled to take. The IRS simply calculates your tax liability based on income and standard deductions.

Even when the IRS does prepare a return it is not considered to be your tax return. Let me explain. The "substitute return" is merely an administrative convenience so that the IRS can assess tax. You can minimize the damaging effect of a Substitute Return by preparing and filing your own return for that same year. You will not avoid the failure to file penalty, but you will in all likelihood reduce the amount of taxes that are owed and interest.

CHAPTER ELEVEN

TAX LIEN

A federal tax lien is a government claim against your property or property interest. The lien may arise when you fail or neglect to pay a tax debt. Its purpose is to protect the government's interest in all of your property both real and personal. This includes bank accounts, retirement accounts, autos, boats, the cash value of life insurance and any other asset in which you have an interest, such as your business.

− A lien is a legal claim to your property used as security or payment for your tax debt and may arise when the tax becomes due and payable.

Hidden Tax Lien

People are aware that a tax lien can be recorded in the county in which you reside. However, most people don't know that the government has a "hidden" tax lien. A tax lien exists when the conditions for it have been met. Even though not recorded, the lien is against all of your property in which you have any interest. In order for a federal tax lien to be valid there are only three requirements:

- The IRS assessed the tax liability
- The IRS gave the taxpayer notice of the assessment and demanded payment

- The taxpayer failed to pay the amount assessed within 10 days of the notice and demand

You can readily see that it doesn't take very long for the government to have a lien against all of your property. Also, once the lien is established, it also attaches to the property you acquire *after* the lien is established.

IRS Has 10 Years to Collect

The IRS is allowed 10 years to collect outstanding tax debt. There are some events that extend this period, such as during the pendency of a bankruptcy proceeding; during the time that an offer in compromise being considered; or, during the time that a collection due process hearing is requested.

Public Notice of Tax Lien

A document recorded in the county recorder's office of the County in which you reside gives constructive notice to the whole world. Constructive notice means that people are presumed to know something because it is published or recorded in a public place. Modernly, recording the notice with the country recorder serves the same purpose. For example, a mortgage lender may not have actual notice of a judgment or lien, but the lender is presumed to have checked for recorded liens against your property. This is called "constructive notice").

To give notice to others who may deal with you (constructive notice), the IRS records a document entitled "Notice of Federal Tax Lien" to alert creditors that the government has a legal right to your property.

Removing a Tax Lien

The obvious way to remove the tax lien is to pay the tax debt in full. Often this may be difficult if not impossible given your circumstances. Other than by payment of the tax, there may be situations in which a tax lien can be lifted or removed. For example, a tax lien can be removed if it can be shown that the IRS's chance of collecting the debt is improved by removing the lien.

Case Study – Tax Lien Removed

Joe is employed in a job that requires that as a condition of employment, that he does not have any tax liens. In other words, he cannot get the job for which he has trained, if he has a federal tax lien. Joe offers proof to the IRS that his salary will be increased sufficiently so that he can not only cover his living expenses, but will also have an improved ability to pay the past-due taxes. The IRS may remove the lien.

Discharge of a Tax Lien

A tax lien may be discharged under several scenarios. If the property is to be sold, but the new buyer requires financing, the tax lien would have priority over the new financing. If there is no equity in the property, the IRS may discharge the tax lien because the taxpayer has no equity in the property.

Subordination of Tax Lien

A tax lien may be subordinated to another creditor if the taxpayer can demonstrate that the government's position is enhanced by the subordination. A subordination of a lien is not the same as a release of lien. The lien remains in effect, but the mortgage is in first position.

Case Study - Subordination

Bundy owns a home on the coast that was severely damaged by a hurricane. The home is worth $100,000 in its damaged condition. Bundy's mortgage on that property is $150,000. He also has a tax lien on the property of $50,000. The bank has agreed to advance Bundy an additional $75,000 to repair the home. Once repaired the home's value will be increased to $275,000, leaving sufficient equity to cover the tax lien. In this case, the IRS may agree to subordinate the tax lien to the new mortgage loan.

CHAPTER TWELVE

LEVY

Unlike a tax lien which gives notice of a tax debt, a levy is the actual seizure of property to satisfy tax debt. If you do not pay your taxes or make arrangements to settle your debt, the IRS may seize and sell any type of personal property or real property that you own, or even property in which you have an interest.

−A levy is a legal seizure of your property to satisfy a tax debt.

For example, the IRS could levy against (seize) property held by someone else. Examples of property in which you have an interest, but that is held for you by someone else include: bank accounts; your retirement account; life insurance policy; and your interest in a partnership or business. These may be levied to pay your tax bill.

If the IRS can show that you transferred property to someone else after a tax lien was in place, the IRS can set-aside the transfer. That is, the IRS can take the property from the other person. If for example, you have a 1967 Camaro that you want to keep until "you can explain things" to the IRS. You transfer the title to the 1967 Camaro to your brother-in-law. The IRS can trace that transfer and seize and sell the Camaro (see Fraudulent Transfers, below).

If there are circumstances putting the government's interest in your assets in jeopardy, the IRS may levy almost immediately (under a jeopardy assessment). A levy requires:

- An assessment of the tax and a notice and demand for payment
- A failure or refusal to pay the tax
- The IRS sends you a "Final Notice of Intent to Levy and Notice of Your Right to a Hearing".

A levy may be released under several different circumstances. If you pay the tax, penalties and interest; the levy will be released. If the time for collection, that is the statute limitations has run on the debt, the levy will be released.

−A levy may be released if the IRS determines that the levy is creating an immediate economic hardship.

Other circumstances in which the levy may be released are: to prove economic hardship; prove that the IRS chances of collection are improved by a release; or, by entering into an installment agreement. Caution, this is not automatic. In some cases the IRS may agree to an installment agreement but does not agree to release the levy. In addition, the levy may be released if you can show that the government's expense of selling your property would be greater than the money realized from the sale of property by the government.

Releasing Seized Property

A release of property seized by the IRS is possible. The IRS may release seized property using an analysis similar to that it uses for lifting a lien. A summary of the main reasons for releasing property after seizure are:

- You pay the amount of the government's interest in the property.
- You enter into an escrow arrangement.
- You post a bond in an amount and from an insurer, which is satisfactory to the government.
- You propose a manner and method of payment of the tax debt that is acceptable to the government.

Returning Levied Property

If the IRS makes a mistake, it may be required to return your property. You have certain due process rights under the 4th Amendment and the Tax Payer Bill of Rights. If a step is missed, it may be enough to require the government to return your property. Examples of the main reasons justifying a return of your property are:

- The IRS levies before it has sent you required notices;
- The IRS acts before your time to respond to a notice has expired; or,
- The IRS did not follow its own internal procedures.

The IRS *may consider* returning property if:

- It agrees to an installment payment arrangement with you;
- Returning the property will help you pay your taxes; or,
- Returning your property is in the best interest of the government.

CHAPTER THIRTEEN

UNDERSTANDING PENALTIES

This is easily the most boring and tedious chapter, but I can't discuss penalties without telling you the about the different penalties that may apply. Have hope. Skim this chapter just deep enough to have a sense that there are different penalties that arise from different kinds of conduct. Later, when you are reading your IRS notice or letter, look for your penalty assessment. These are usually stated on the second or third page of the notice. With the notice in front of you, return to this chapter, and find you penalty. It will make much more sense to you at that time than it will on a first read.

There are varieties of penalties that arise from not filing a tax return or not paying the tax bill. Penalties can be both civil and criminal. The civil penalties can increase if the IRS determines that your conduct was willful and not merely negligent. In a general sense, penalties will be calculated from the date a return must be filed, in other words its "due date".

   – Penalties are assessed for late filing, late payment and may be assessed because of inaccuracy, willful negligence and frivolous tax returns

Income Tax Return Due Dates

The Internal Revenue Code requires every taxpayer to file a return of tax by a certain date each year. Failure to file by the due date triggers a late filing penalty.

- Personal taxes on form 1040 are due April 15 of each year.
- Partnership returns on form 1065 are due April 15.
- Corporate returns (for both C corporations and S corporations) are due on the 15th day of the 3rd month after the end of the corporation's tax year. For most corporations, the end of the tax year will be December 31 and the return is due March 15.

All due dates that fall on a weekend or holiday (or occasionally when federal offices are otherwise closed in Washington D.C.), the due date is the next business day. Taxpayers may request a tax year that ends other than the end of the calendar year, but you are required upon a showing of good cause to apply for approval from the Commissioner of the Internal Revenue before using a fiscal year instead of the calendar year.

Please keep in mind that here we are only discussing income tax return dates in this book. There are different kinds of tax returns, as, for example, estate taxes, gift taxes, payroll taxes and excise taxes. Some returns are required to be filed quarterly. If you have to file one of these returns, you can obtain from the IRS web site a tax calendar, or refer to IRS Publication 506 for information about when these returns are due.

Payment of Taxes on Due Date

Taxes are due and payable on the date that the return is required to be filed. Some people delay filing because they believe that, by not filing, they can put off being billed by the IRS. However, the duty to file and the duty to pay the taxes due are separate and each carries a separate penalty.

Required Estimated Tax Payments

In addition, if you owed taxes last year then you are required to estimate the taxes that will be due this year and make quarterly deposits. The total of your deposits must be within 10% of the actual tax due for the year. If this requirement is not met, you are assessed an underpayment penalty.

Case Study

Sally is retired. She served in the military for 20 years and has income from her military retirement which is not disability related. DFAS withholds a portion for taxes. Sally also has investment income from stocks, some of which are actively traded by her Broker. As a result of fluctuations in the market, her investment income is variable from year to year. Nevertheless, she must estimate this income within 10% or suffer an underpayment penalty. She avoids the penalty by estimating her tax for the current year by dividing her total tax liability from last year by four, and making a quarterly payment to the IRS, using IRS form 1040-V.

Extensions for Filing and Payment

The IRS will automatically grant an extension to file to individual taxpayers. This extension permits delaying filing a form 1040 until October 15 of the same year. Because the extension is automatic, all you will need to do is to file IRS form 4868 which can be mailed or filed electronically. If you file for an extension by mail, you will not receive any confirmation from the IRS. Therefore, you will have no proof that you actually made a timely application to extend your filing date.

*– An extension to file a return is <u>not</u> an extension to pay the tax due
for that year*

When filed electronically, the IRS will send you an acknowledgment or confirmation number. Keep this confirmation number in case of a subsequent question about whether you actually applied for the automatic extension. If a paid tax preparer files for an extension on your behalf, the preparer should provide you with the confirmation number he or she received electronically from the IRS. An extension for a longer period of time is possible; but, you must make a separate application to the IRS and show a need to extend the due date for a longer period.

You should be aware that an extension to file is not an extension to pay. Said another that way, if you obtain an extension to file, the taxes are still due on the original due date regardless of when the extension filing date occurs. An extension to *file* is different from an extension to *pay*.

Case study - Extension to File

Ricky is filing his tax return as unmarried, but he is unable to get all of his documentation together before the April 15 deadline. He applies for and obtains the automatic extension to file until October 15. He completes his return in October and files it on October 15, owing $1250.

The $1250 tax, figured in October, was due and payable by April 15 even though his return had not been prepared at that time, and he did not know the correct amount of tax until October. Ricky is assessed a late payment penalty. Interest on the tax is computed from April 15. He could have avoided the penalty by making a good faith estimate of his tax and paying it using IRS form 1040-V on or before April 15.

Failure to File Penalty

Filing a tax return on the due date (or extension date) is not optional. Often heard excuses for not filing on time include:

- "I do not understand the forms"
- "I lost my paperwork"
- "I was getting a divorce and didn't know what I was supposed to file"
- "I didn't file last year so I was afraid to file this year"

Sorry, but none of the above excuses will work. True, late filing penalties can be abated if "good cause" is shown, but these excuses are not sufficient. The failure to file penalty (which includes late filing) is painful to your pocket book. The penalty is 5% of the tax due for each month, or part of a month, the return is late up to a maximum of 25%. The penalty is based on the portion of the tax that has not been paid.

If your failure to file is due to fraud, the penalty is 15% for each month, or part of a month, that you return is late. The maximum penalty is 75% of the unpaid tax.

Failure to Pay Penalty

Paying the taxes late, that is after the due date, results in a second kind of penalty. The failure to file penalty is 1/2 of 1% (0.5%) of your unpaid taxes *for each month*, or part of a month, after the due date the taxes not paid. This penalty does not apply if you paid at least 90% of the taxes due on or before the filing date.

⇨ See the section on "Required Estimated Payments", above.

Penalty Rate Increases after Demand or Levy Notice

Once the IRS issues a notice of intent to Levy, the late payment penalty increases to 1% (from .05%), effectively doubling the penalty. Remember this is the rate for each month. The same is true if a notice and demand for immediate payment is issued. In this case the increased rate begins at the start of the first month after the notice demand was issued.

Combined Penalties

If both the failure to file penalty and the failure to pay penalty apply in any month, the 5% failure to file penalty is reduced by the failure to pay penalty. It is important to note that if you file your return more than 60 days late, the minimum penalty is the smaller of $135 or *100% of the unpaid tax*.

Accuracy Related Penalty

Occasionally someone will just throw numbers onto their tax return just so they can file something before the due date. This is not a good strategy. If there is no basis for the representations made, then an "accuracy related penalty" can also apply equal to 20% of any underpayment of tax. The accuracy related penalty applies if:

- You show negligence or disregard of the rules and regulations;
- You substantially understate your income tax; or,
- You claim tax benefits for transaction that lacks economic substance.

The penalty is equal to 20% of the underpayment but can rise to 40% of the underpayment that is attributable to an undisclosed non-economic substantive transaction or undisclosed foreign financial asset transaction.

– A fabricated statement or false information on your return increases penalties and may result in audits for multiple years. Criminal penalties are possible.

I know this is a little complicated. The take away for you is to remember that a fabricated tax return can substantially increase your penalties. You will want to be sure that you have real transactions and real financial information on any tax return that you sign.

⇨ See the section in this chapter on "Frivolous Tax Submission".

Case Study

Shelly ran out of time to have her taxes prepared by someone else. On April 15 (the last day to file a return without a penalty) she starts to prepare her own tax return. She uses a well-known online tax return preparation web application. Shelly does not have all of her records together. Nevertheless, she enters information in the various screens of the web application. Since she does not have her tax records, she "makes up" some of what she enters into the web app. The web app checks her returns and reports there are no errors. She then eFiles her return before midnight on April 15. Shelly congratulates herself for avoiding the failure to file penalty.

In August, Shelly receives a notice from the IRS that there were substantial understatements of income and overstatements of expenses. The IRS gives notice that it intends to assess the Accuracy Related Penalty and the Frivolous Tax Submission Penalty. Shelly will owe the penalty assessments if the IRS could have reasonably concluded that Shelly was willfully careless in preparing her tax return.

Frivolous Tax Submission

A frivolous tax submission is one that does not include enough information to figure the correct tax. A return that contains information that clearly shows that the tax you reported is substantially incorrect is also frivolous. If the IRS deems your return "frivolous" you may have to pay a penalty of $5000 for each frivolous return filed.

Interest

In addition to all of the types of penalties that may apply, they IRS will also charge interest on the unpaid tax balance. The federal government determines quarterly a short-term interest rate. The interest assessed on a tax balance is the sum of the short term rate plus 3%. For example, as of this writing the federal short-term rate is .28%. This is a very low rate. If the economy changes the rate can go up substantially. Federal short-term rates in excess of 6% are known.

A Good Excuse for Abatement

Abatement is the removal or reduction in the penalties assessed. The IRS may grant penalty abatement upon a showing of reasonable cause. Unfortunately, the burden of proving "reasonableness" falls on you, the taxpayer. There is no abatement possible for the estimated tax penalty.

To obtain abatement, you are required to show ordinary business care and prudence. This standard requires you to attempt to meet the filing or payment requirements as soon as possible. Making a late payment at the earliest opportunity that you can manage may help you establish that the failure to pay was due to reasonable cause and not willful neglect. Be aware that ordinary circumstances such as being in a divorce, losing financial documents and the like will not be sufficient, without more, to obtain an abatement of penalty.

Case Study

Joe and his wife Kaylie had their taxes prepared at a well-known retail chain tax preparation service. They were told they could take certain credits relating to child care. The advice was incorrect, and they were assessed additional tax as well as failure to pay penalty.

Later, their attorney made a written request for waiver of the penalty based on reasonable cause. The request was granted and the penalty waived because they had taken ordinary care and prudence by seeking the help of a tax preparer, and, had in good faith relied on the advice received from the tax preparer.

There are also other considerations that will result in a waiver of penalties. For example, in tax litigation the IRS may abate a penalty to help settle a case under a "hazards of litigation" analysis. This means that IRS counsel has determined that there is some chance that the taxpayer's attorney will win in Tax Court. Weighing the risks of litigation vs. the benefit of an agreed tax amount, the IRS may make a business decision to settle for less than the amount claimed to be owed.

Civil Fraud Penalties – 75% Whoa!

Tax evasion can have both civil and criminal sanctions. Even if taxcpayer avoids criminal prosecution, the IRS may assess a civil fraud penalty. The penalty is up to 75% of the underpayment of the tax attributable to the fraud, *plus* the taxes owed.

– Investors can be hit with civil fraud penalties in abusive tax shelters

Promoters of securities or investments are creative. A common thread is the sale of an "investment" that has a large tax write-off. Frequently the investment object, whether it is a gold mine in the jungle or oil exploration in Oklahoma, should raise suspicions if the prospectus promises large tax write-offs or deductions for investors.

Investors, particularly with regard to private offerings, have a duty to exercise due diligence before investing in these schemes. An investor's failure to inquire may lead to a civil fraud penalty. If it looks too good to be true, have it reviewed by your CPA or tax attorney. Given the substantial risks, a couple of hours of attorney time are well worth the expense.

Criminal Penalties

Certain types of conduct are treated as crimes for which there can be actual jail time, in addition to severe financial penalties. The IRS has a criminal investigations division (CID) that investigates tax fraud, tax evasion and other tax crimes. When appropriate, CID recommends criminal prosecution to the Department of Justice. DOJ referrals and tax crimes are beyond the scope of this book. Here is a short list of the kinds of things that can trigger criminal liability:

- Tax evasion
- Willful failure to file a return
- Willful failure to supply information
- Willful failure or refusal to pay any tax due
- Making false or fraudulent statements to the IRS
- Preparing and filing a fraudulent return
- Identity theft

Jail time is a possibility. In lieu of, or in addition to jail time, a promoter of an abusive tax shelter scheme can also face a financial penalty of up to $250,000. The number of ways that people attempt tax evasion is only limited by human imagination. Below is one example.

Case Study – Tax Evasion by General Contractor

A Colorado contractor was sentenced to 71 months in prison and 5 years of supervised probation plus $60,597 in restitution to the IRS.

His crime? He was a general contractor focused on roofing and remodeling. He also was an investor in residential real estate, essentially flipping homes. From 2005 – 2008 he wilfully attempted to evade both income tax and payroll tax. To conceal his income, he established and used trusts diverting $90,000 in deposits. In addition there was an attempt to defraud a lender by using fraudulent treasury checks for his benefit.

CHAPTER FOURTEEN

PAYMENT OPTIONS

It is in your best interest to pay taxes when due because the balance is subject to interest and a monthly late payment penalty. Even if you cannot pay the total amount due, pay a portion to help reduce the accumulation of additional charges.

– You are always better off to pay something, even a small amount, than to completely ignore tax debt

You can pay the balance due on your personal tax return with a check or money order made payable to the "United States Treasury" with you return. Do not send cash. The IRS would prefer that you fill out form 1040-V to accompany the check. I recommend that, in the lower left margin of the check (on the memo line), you write your Social Security number, the year for which you are paying, and the form number of the return. For individuals, the tax form is the familiar 1040.

Example of what to write on memo line of a check:

123-45-6789 2014 1040

Debit and Credit Card Payments

Another option is to pay by debit or credit card. The IRS provides a list of third-party providers they will accept your credit card or debit card and remit your payment to the Department of the Treasury. Each of these providers will charge a fee for their services, and some maintain a live operator. There is a link on the IRS web site, but the page changes from time to time. If you want to use one of these services it is recommended that you navigate to the IRS website (www.IRS.gov) and search for "credit card payment".

Electronic Federal Tax Payment System

There is a method of payment that many taxpayers don't know about, EFTPS. You can make electronic payments to your tax account online. The service is free, unlike credit card payments. Best of all, you can make a payment in any amount that you can manage. For example, you could pay $20 a week, if that suited your circumstances.

To use this service you must enroll using your tax payer identification number (usually your SSAN). You also need to have a bank account from which the EFTPS system can debit your account. The funds will not be moved out of your bank account until the date you select for settlement.

– Use EFTPS to debit your bank account online or by telephone. Enroll at https://www.eftps.gov/eftps/

Installment Agreements

You may be able to obtain an installment agreement with the IRS. This will allow you to pay any back taxes monthly over a fixed period. During the time that you have an installment agreement, tax refunds from future years will be applied to the remaining balance. In addition to being able to pay over time, the advantage of the installment agreement is that the IRS will suspend enforcement activity during the life of the installment agreement.

To be eligible you must have filed all past-due tax returns and complete IRS form 9465 "Installment Agreement Request". In addition, the IRS may require you to complete form 433-F "Collection Information Statement". You will also have to pay a fee for setting up your installment agreement. The changes changes from time to time, but is currently $52 for a direct debit agreement or $120 for a standard agreement or payroll deduction agreement.

Summary of Basic Requirements:

- File all tax returns past due or currently due
- Complete and submit your financial information on IRS form 433-F (sometimes this is not required, as for example streamlined or fresh start programs)
- Complete and submit a request for an installment agreement on IRS form 9465
- Pay an administrative fee determined by the IRS

The Collection Information Statement (433-F) is a bit tricky. In this statement you are required to disclose all of your income, all of your liabilities (including the name of your creditors) and all assets. The reason that this is a bit tricky is that you cannot lie and must be completely truthful.

If you should later default on an installment agreement or there should be another tax year in which liability becomes due, the IRS can use all of the information in the Collection Information Statement to locate assets to seize and bank accounts to levy.

– Without lying, use the 433-F to paint a picture of what you can afford to pay monthly. Giving false information is a crime.

In addition to the 433-F, the IRS will likely ask for supporting documentation. Expect to provide three months of bank statements and recent paystubs. If you have a car loan you will be asked to provide a recent bill showing the payment and the balance owing. If you own your home, you will be asked to provide a mortgage statement; and, if you rent, a copy of a rent statement. If you have high medical expenses, you will also be required to provide bills or invoices from your medical service provider and pharmacy.

Review of Proposed Installment Agreement

An IRS manager must review a request for an installment agreement that falls outside of the streamlined agreement initiative. Before accepting your request the IRS will consider:

- Whether you have failed to file within the past five years any tax return;
- Whether you have failed to pay any tax due; or,
- Whether you have entered into a prior installment agreement.

In addition, the IRS must determine that you are unable to pay the liability in full based on the information that you provided in the Collection Information Statement. Not all hope is lost, however. A tax attorney may be able to negotiate an installment agreement even if you do not otherwise qualify for the program.

Streamlined (Fresh Start) Installment Agreement

From time to time, the IRS offers new initiatives to help its public image. Often these "new" initiatives are recycled old initiatives that are changed slightly. The current initiative is called "Fresh Start" a feature of which is a Streamlined Installment Agreement. If the total that you owe (tax, penalty and interest) is less than $25,000 (this amount can change and may be up to $50,000 in some situations) you can apply online. Under this program you may not be required to fill out the complete Collection Information Statement. However, you will be required to provide some financial information.

A requirement of any installment agreements is that all prior tax returns must be filed before the agreement can be accepted by the IRS. In addition, you will be required to enroll in a direct debit or payroll deduction arrangement with the IRS, as previously mentioned.

– Before agreeing to a payroll deduction, check with your employer

There are issues to consider with either a direct debit or payroll deduction. Some employers will refuse to do the payroll deduction because of the time, cost and additional bookkeeping required. The employer cannot be compelled to withhold and remit the withholdings to the IRS. Therefore check with your employer before you agree to a payroll deduction arrangement.

In regard to direct debit payment arrangements, you must be sure that there is money in the account to cover the IRS automatic debit to your account. If there are insufficient funds to cover one payment, your agreement is technically in default. My experience has been that the IRS will work with you, but you will need to take the initiative to telephone. If there is a pattern of missed payments, such as multiple insufficient funds notices, the IRS will take action. When the installment agreement is in default the IRS may terminate the agreement and resume its collection efforts, usually by a wage levy.

CHAPTER FIFTEEN

OFFER IN COMPROMISE

An offer in compromise is an agreement in which the government agrees to accept less than the full amount owed in full settlement of your tax debt. The essential feature is a compromise that is in the best interest of both the taxpayer and the government. To be considered, you must make an appropriate offer based on what the IRS considers your true ability to pay.

– An offer in compromise allows you to settle your tax debt for less than the full amount you owe.

Settle for Pennies on the Dollar - Fact or Fiction?

I know that you have heard advertisements every day on the TV and on the radio in which a slick sounding actor tells says "YOU can settle your tax case for only pennies on the dollar". The taglines for the ads include:

- Taxes owed $50,000, settled for $100
- Owed $100,000, actually paid $5000
- John and Mary settled for pennies on the dollar
- Susan owed $26,000, but our tax experts were able to settle for $26

Are these factual claims, or are they purely fiction? When you hear one of these ads, treat it with a healthy amount of skepticism. The majorities of tax firms are reputable and deliver value and good service.

However, there are many instances in which the business provide little service and run a boiler room call center, the main purpose of which is to sign new customers. Some nationally known businesses have been sanctioned or even sued by state attorney generals or state consumer protection division. The advertisements are used to scoop up leads. When a taxpayer telephones, they are connected to "associates" who are actually sales reps. Sales reps may be paid a commission to sign up the taxpayer.

– Most tax representation services are reputable businesses

There is good news. It is true that some taxpayers are able to get amazing settlements. Please notice that I said "some". Not everyone qualifies. Even people who might qualify are rejected because of an unskilled attempt to negotiate settlement. Qualifying clients have been able to settle for extremely low sums, literally pennies on the dollar.

You, however, should avoid unreasonable expectations. Although many accepted compromise agreements significantly reduce tax liability, few actually settle for pennies. The key element is to establish that you cannot pay the full amount of your tax and the likelihood your being able to do so in the future is doubtful.

Case Study – Successful Offer In Compromise

Geoff and Shandra had 7 years of unfiled tax returns. In some years, they had filed as "married filing jointly" and some years they had filed as "married filing separately". They had tax liability (owed taxes) for most of these years. In addition, Geoff had owned a small business 6 years ago, but did not make his payroll tax deposits. In total, Geoff was liable for $120,000 in back taxes while Shandra's tax liability was $35,000. I was able to settle each of the three different tax liabilities, for all years, for $500 each, a total of $1,500.

If your offer in compromise is accepted, the traditional requirement is to pay the entire offer amount immediately. The IRS has now made this a bit easier. Payment can be made 20% upfront submitted with the offer and 80% within 90 days of acceptance. Also, the IRS may accept a short-term deferred payment over 24 months. If you offer is rejected, the payment made with the offer is not returned to you. Instead, it is applied to reduce your tax balance.

The IRS accepts only about 34% of all offers in compromise of tax debt. For most people, an offer in compromise will likely be unsuccessful. In my opinion, much of the television and radio advertising is, in fact, misleading because it implies results, that cannot be obtained for everyone. Take note of the very small print at the bottom of the TV screen that flashes by faster than it can be read. In the text will be words that say something like "if you qualify". Beware.

Nevertheless, it is useful in every tax case to at least consider the possibility of making an offer in compromise. A successful offer in compromise is not a matter of blind luck or even throwing darts. The are rules can be applied by a competent tax professional experienced in making settlement offers. Our office has considerably better success rate than the national statistics. This is large part accomplished by making honest realistic assessments of a client's options, including offers in compromise.

The Eligibility Process

There is a process for making an offer in compromise. The process includes evaluation and verification by the IRS, taking into account and giving consideration to, any special circumstances that may affect your ability to pay. Said another way, if you are currently able to pay the taxes owed, it is unlikely that the IRS will accept your offer.

Before you can make an offer, you must file all tax returns that are currently due or past-due. In addition, if estimated tax payments are required for the current year, these must be current. If you are a business owner with employees, you must have made all required federal tax deposits for the current quarter.

Bankruptcy

If you are in bankruptcy, the IRS will not enter into an offer in compromise. When a bankruptcy petition is filed, all IRS collection activities must cease until your case is dismissed or discharged. The bankruptcy trustee has complete control of your assets. The trustee's goal is to liquidate assets so as to have funds to pay possible creditors, which includes the IRS.

⇨ See the chapter, "Bankruptcy to Reduce Tax Debt".

Doubt as to Liability

Doubt as to liability is a legal argument. It requires legal analysis of statutory and case law. If your tax attorney can persuade the IRS that there is "doubt as to liability", the IRS may accept an offer in compromise, in situations in which the offer would otherwise be rejected.

Doubt as to liability exist where there is a genuine dispute as to the existence or amount of the correct tax liability under the law. Doubt as to liability does not exist where liability has been established by a final court decision or judgment concerning the existence or amount of the tax liability.

Doubt as to Collectability

Doubt as to Collectability is a factual argument and is a factor weighing in favor of persuading the IRS to accept your offer. To establish doubt as to collectability, the IRS evaluates your personal financial profile. Your income less your allowable expenses (living, housing and transportation) as well as the liquidity of assets or the availability of credit. For example, if you have a 30 foot luxury boat that is fully paid for, the IRS would ask you to sell the boat and apply the proceeds to your tax debt before it would consider an offer in compromise. If you have equity in real estate, the IRS will expect to sell or borrow on the property to pay down your taxes, before it will approve an offer in compromise.

CHAPTER SIXTEEN

INNOCENT SPOUSE

Joint and Several Liability

Innocent spouse relief, as it is often called, is the relief from joint and several liability for taxes. Let's break that down. When you file your income tax return using the filing status of "Married Filing Jointly", you and your spouse are equally liable for the taxes due on the return. Let's be clear here. Your liability is not ½ of the tax. You are liable for the *entire* amount of tax on the return. If your spouse skips out, the IRS can collect the entire amount from you.

But I Didn't Sign the Return!

The IRS could impose joint and several liability, even if you did not sign the return. Really? Well, yes. The inquiry will be whether you intended the return to be your joint return.

Case Study

> Randall and Kandy use an online web application to prepare their 2013 tax return. Kandy is better with taxes than Randall, so she does the actual return while Randall takes the kids to their soccer match. Kandy completes the return and e-Files it using a service provided by the software company. When Randall returns, Kandy tells him

she filed the return. Randall says to her "I'm glad we got that done. I can't wait for the refund."

Randall did not sign the return, but he is jointly and severally liable. This is because he intended the return to be the couple's joint return.

It is possible to contest an electronic signature by extrinsic facts. For example, if in the above case study Kandy had in prior years always filed their returns separately, that fact would be a factor in determine whether there was joint liability.

Randall could avoid liability if his signature was forged. Also, if he had signed the return under duress he could avoid joint liability. Duress can be shown by external facts showing a physically or psychologically abusive spouse.

Eligibility for Innocent Spouse Relief

You can request the IRS to grant you innocent spouse relief. If the IRS agrees, you will be relieved of responsibility for paying tax, interest and penalties. The IRS will thereafter only be able to collect from the other spouse.

To qualify for innocent spouse relief you must show the following:

- You filed a joint return.
- The tax on the return was understated.
- When you signed the return, you did not know and had no reason to know that the taxes on the return were understated.
- Taking into account all the facts and circumstances, it would not be equitable to hold you responsible.

Let me explain what the IRS means by "understated". An understatement is when the taxes owed are greater than what was actually shown on the return. An understate can result when a deductible item or capital loss is disallowed.

Case Study

Joe and Maria are married. Joe prepared their 2014 income tax return and took a large loss from an investment partnership. In the previous year, a promoter had persuaded Joe to invest in a gold mine in Brazil. The investment was a sham, because the mine did not operate and its sole purpose was to generate tax losses for the investors.

Maria did not know about the investment in the gold mine. Moreover, she never saw the tax return that Joe prepared. When the fake loss was disallowed, the IRS determined that there was an understatement because the correct tax was higher than what was shown on the income tax return.

Separation of Liability Relief

There is another way to obtain relief. It is not complete relief; instead the liability is allocated between you and your former spouse. This type of relief is only available for taxes that are unpaid. If you have a refund this approach will not apply to you.

The requirements for separation of liability relief are:

- You are no longer married, living apart or are a widow.
- You were not a member of the same household as you ex-spouse for at least the 12 months prior to requesting relief.
- You were without actual knowledge of the erroneous item.
- There was not a fraudulent transfer of property between you and your ex-spouse

See the Section in this chapter on Fraudulent Transfers

Even though there is not complete relief from taxes, having to pay only a portion of the tax is a big help. Remember, that otherwise you are jointly liable for the *full* amount of taxes on your return. If the liability can be apportioned to just the portion for which you are responsible, for you have sucessfully acomplished a great deal.

Case Study

Jan and Dean were married when they filed their joint income tax return for 2013. The next year they separated and lived apart for the full year. Unknown to Jan, Dean had significant gambling winnings in 2013. These winnings were not reported on their joint tax return. Because Jan did not know about the unreported income; he was granted relief and the IRS apportioned the tax liability, cutting his tax liability by 60%.

Equitable Relief

There is a third means of obtaining relief from joint liability for taxes, interest and penalties. In this type of relief the IRS attempts to balance the equities by looking at the particular facts of your case.

There is a long list of factors that the IRS will consider. The main points include:

- You did not have actual knowledge of omitted income or an erroneous item.
- There is fault (ex. you gave you spouse money to pay the tax, but he went shopping instead of actually paying the tax).
- You did not file your return with the intent to commit fraud.
- Whether you were living apart, separated or divorced.
- Whether you were subject to physical or mental abuse.

Tax Relief: One Size Does Not Fit All

In this chapter we have only discussed the main points for each of the ways in which you may obtain innocent spouse relief. Our goal is make the principles understandable without burdening you with too much detail. Innocent spouse relief is definitely not a "one size fits all" topic. Most tax payers only apply for Equitable Relief, probably because the IRS provides a form that you can fill out and easily submit (IRS form 8857).

I suggest that you weigh your options carefully. Think about how the concepts for showing a reason for relief apply to your individual circumstances. Write a draft, set it aside, and review it later. You will want to be sure that it explains your case in a way that makes sense to the IRS employee who will read it. Keep in mind that relief requires that you show the IRS a combination of factors that support each other.

CHAPTER SEVENTEEN

APPEALS

Appeals Office

The Appeals Office is separate and independent from the IRS. However, the employees that are working in appeals are IRS employees. The Appeals Officers have experience either in tax auditing or collections, having worked in those areas before coming to the Appeals Office. Therefore, you should keep in mind that the Appeals personnel have a mindset towards collection. Nevertheless, they will attempt to be fair and neutral in the application of the Internal Revenue Code to your facts and circumstances.

Tax Dispute

A tax dispute arises when the IRS makes a determination adverse to your interest, and you disagree. Most determinations are subject to administrative appeal and usually fall into two categories, deficiencies and collection issues.

A deficiency appeal is available when the IRS increases your taxable income after examination. This appeal may include deficiency penalties that are computed as a percentage of the deficiency and tax. Certain collection actions may also be administratively appealed.

These arise if the Collection Division proposes to take, or has taken, certain actions to collect on an assessment. You may also appeal an IRS decision denying you an "offer in compromise" or when the IRS has, or is planning to, revoke an installment agreement that is already in place.

To be eligible for an appeal, you must have received a letter from the IRS explaining your right to appeal the IRS's decision, you must disagree with the decision and you do not sign an agreement to waive your appeals right. The waiver is included with the letter and is presented in a way that a taxpayer might construe to mean that the taxpayer must sign the waiver.

To summarize your right to appeal administratively:

- The IRS has given you notice that you have a right to appeal an adverse decision;
- You have a reason to disagree with the decision; and,
- You do not consent to waive your appeal rights.

– Inaction will result in a waiver of your right to appeal an IRS decision. The time allowed to respond may be short.

Please note that your time to appeal is limited and can be time barred by inaction. The time in which you had to respond is stated in the Notice that you receive. If you do not request an appeal and file a protest within the time stated, you are barred from appealing a deficiency assessment. When your appeal is time barred the IRS might levy, take another collection action or terminate an installment agreement, if you had one in place.

Notice of Deficiency Waiver

In a deficiency appeal, the IRS will ask you to sign a Notice of Deficiency Waiver. The waiver can come in any one of a number of different IRS forms or letters. If you sign a waiver, the IRS is permitted to assess the tax shown as due. In most cases, it is not a good idea to sign this form because the assessment triggers penalties and interest.

You are not eligible to appeal if the letter that you receive from the IRS was only a bill for taxes due. If there was an audit of your account and you did not provide all of the information to support your position to the tax examiner, you are not eligible to appeal. If your only concern is that you cannot pay the amount of the tax assessed, then you do not have a right to an appeal.

Collection Due Process Hearing

A Collection Due Process hearing does not replace the collection appeals process, but supplements it. It is intended to provide a forum for a review of your due process rights in collection matters. The law requires the IRS to send you a written notice no more than five days after the government files a Notice of Federal Tax Lien that states the amount of unpaid tax and informs you of your right to an administrative appeal.

The CDP procedures also provide for expedited review of levies. Notice must be sent to the taxpayer no less than 30 days before the levy is to occur. The notice informs you of your right to request a hearing within 30 days of the notice.

The 30 day time limit is strict and if missed, bars your right to a CDP review or to take the matter later to court. You have 30 days to file a "Request for a Collection Due Process or Equivalent Hearing". If you miss the deadline you still have a right to request an "Equivalency" hearing. This is less desirable because the Appeals Office considers fewer issues than it does in a CDP hearing. Nevertheless, it is an option that you should consider. A CDP hearing is not expedited, meaning it may take months to obtain a hearing and review. However, collection activity is suspended during the pendency of the hearing. A suspension is double edged because the statute of limitations period is extended by the time it takes for Appeals to render a decision on your CDP request.

Representation

You may have an attorney or representative appear on your behalf at your appeals hearing or conference. Your representative must be one who is enrolled to practice before the IRS and to whom you have given your power of attorney to represent you before the IRS.

Take note that your tax preparer may not be able to represent you in an appeal. A tax preparer, even one with a PTIN or a person calling himself or herself a "registered preparer", is not authorized to represent you before the IRS. Only attorneys, CPAs or enrolled agents are recognized.

Appeals Hearing Not Available

In some situations, an appeals hearing is not available to the taxpayer. The Appeals Office does not have jurisdiction to hear any case in which:

- Criminal prosecution is pending;
- Criminal Prosecution Is Not Fully Completed; or,

- "Tax Protester" cases in which the taxpayer refuses to comply with the tax law on religious, political or constitutional grounds.

CHAPTER EIGHTEEN

TAKE THE IRS TO COURT

Tax Court

The U.S. Tax Court is an Article I court established by Congress. The court provides a forum for taxpayers to have their case decided without having to first pay the tax that the IRS claims is due. This is a big advantage because other courts require that the tax be paid before these other courts have jurisdiction to hear your tax case.

In Tax Court, your case is started by filing a Petition with the court. The Petition must be timely filed, or it will be barred. The Tax Court has 19 appointed judges and other special trial judges who travel during the year to various designated cities to conduct trials. This is a great convenience because you do not have to travel to a Washington D.C. to have the Tax Court hear your case. In cases involving $50,000 or less, the Tax Court offers a small tax case process which is simpler than regular tax case procedures and of great benefit to many taxpayers.

When You Can File a Petition in Tax Court

You are able to Petition the Tax Court to have your case heard when you have received either a Notice of Deficiency or a Notice of Determination from the IRS. You have 90 days from the date of the notice to file your Tax Court petition. If you have not filed your Tax Court petition within the 90 day period the Tax Court no longer has subject matter jurisdiction over your case. If this happens, the tax will be assessed and the government can pursue collection of the tax.

Simple Rules to Remember about filing your case in tax court:
- You must have received a Notice of Deficiency; or,
- You must have received a Notice of Determination;
- You may be elgible for simpler small case treatment if your case is less than $50,000; and,
- You must file within the 90 limitation period

Working with the IRS Does Not Extend the 90 Day Limitation

Taxpayers naturally want to avoid trouble. Often a taxpayer, having received a notice of deficiency, will try to resolve their matter directly with the IRS. They may telephone, write letters and send documents. They may have one or more telephone or in person discussions with an IRS employee about their case. This is a good thing. I recommend people to be proactive.

However, because of communications with the IRS, the taxpayer may be lulled into believing that they have additional time to file a petition in Tax Court. Not so. It is important to know that your efforts to resolve your case do not extend the time to file your Tax Court petition. Said another way, even though you're trying to work out your solution with the IRS, the clock continues to tick. If you do not file before the end of the 90 days, you lose the right to go to Tax Court.

–The 90 day limit is strictly enforced

Sometimes, taxpayers consciously choose to let the 90 day period expire. This is usually because there is no question as to the amount owed and all that is needed is a payment plan or other work out. In other instances, the amount of the tax change is relatively small in comparison to the cost of litigation, that the case is not pursued in court for economic reasons.

District Court and Courts of Federal Claims

You can also take your case to the District Court or the Court of Federal Claims. The U.S. Court of Federal Claims is authorized to hear money claims against the United States. This court has jurisdiction nationwide. A large part of its workload is tax refund suits. The court is located in Washington D.C. The other court available to you is the U.S. District Court. The District Courts are the trial courts for the U.S. and are located in 94 Districts. There is at least one District Court sitting in each state.

– You must pay the tax asserted by the IRS before the court can hear your case

To proceed in these courts, you must first pay the taxes assessed or claimed by the IRS and then filed a claim for refund with the IRS. Usually you must wait for the IRS to deny your refund claim. There is an exception to this requirement. If you make a claim for refund and the IRS does not respond within six months, you may file suit immediately in either the District Court or the Court of Federal Claims. There is also a time limitation. You must file your suit no later than two years from the date that the IRS disallows your claim for refund.

Litigation in either of these courts is daunting for an unrepresented taxpayer. The courts require strict adherence to the rules of court, the Federal Rules of Civil Procedure and the Federal Rules of Evidence. There will be mandatory conferences, discovery orders and perhaps motions that will require the filing of responses to keep your case from being dismissed. These factors make these courts an impractical choice for a claimant who represents himself or herself.

CHAPTER NINETEEN

TAX PAYER RIGHTS

This is a very short chapter. In fact it is the shortest chapter in the book. You may have heard the media or others speak of the Taxpayer Bill of Rights as if it were something different and apart from the Internal Revenue Code. Today that is not so much the case, but it did start out that way.

Because of wide spread public complaints about IRS abuses Congress decided that it needed to address the problem of perceived abuses by the IRS in its collections practices. There were hearings; speeches were made; and there were elections to be won. Eventually the 1998 Taxpayer Reform Act emerged.

Over the subsequent years, Congress passed multiple pieces of legislation with the title "Taxpayer Bill of Rights". These are sometimes referred to as Taxpayer Bill of Rights I, II and III, each layering upon previous versions.

The various versions articulate changes that Congress wanted to make for taxpayers to contest assessment and curb abusive collection of tax. In addition, Congress created new programs and initiatives which include the Tax Payer Advocate Service and Low Income Taxpayer Clinics. The Internal Revenue Code has been modified to include these additional rights. To conform to the new laws, the IRS changed its policies and procedures. These statutory rights granted by the various reform acts are discussed throughout this book.

These are significant rights that offer more protections than before the passage of the several taxpayer bills of rights. Some of the "rights" not mentioned elsewhere include:

- The right for a taxpayer to have an attorney or properly authorized representative present during any interview;
- The right to suspend an interview so that a taxpayer may consult with an attorney before continuing the interview; and,
- The taxpayer does not have to appear at any interview. He or she can have an attorney or properly authorized representative appear in the taxpayer's place (unless a summons is first served).

Please note that various states have also enacted their own taxpayer rights, which may also be referred to as the Tax Payer Bill of Rights. In this book, we are only discussing your federal rights.

CHAPTER TWENTY

STATUTE OF LIMITATIONS

A statute of limitation is a legal limit on how long the IRS has to make an assessment of tax or collection. When we speak of a limitation period, there are two dates with which we are concerned. First, we need to know when the limitation period began to run. Second, we need to know when the limitation period expires. For the purposes of this book, the limitation period begins to run on the date that the return is due, or if it was filed late, on the date that the return is actually filed. Note that an extension of time to file does not extend the statute limitations date.

Assessment

In order to understand the IRS statute of limitations you need to understand the difference between an *assessment* and a *collection*. An assessment is when the IRS determines that a tax is due. An automatic assessment is authorized and made on the amount of tax shown on your return. A deficiency assessment is made upon examination or audit. Before audit change can become taxes due, the IRS must first send you a Notice of Deficiency. There are certain due process requirements and appeals rights that are triggered by the deficiency notice. Once the time allowed for you to respond or appeal has expired; or, you have taken an appeal and have exhausted your administrative remedy; the deficiency amount is assessed.

Three Year Rule on Assessment

The general rule is that the IRS has three years to make an assessment of tax. If the assessment is made beyond the three-year period and if there are no applicable exceptions, then the assessment is void. If the assessment is void, the IRS is prohibited from collecting on the late assessment.

Exceptions to the Three Year Rule on Assessment

Every general rule has its exception, and that is especially true in taxation cases. Below is a summary of the most common exceptions encountered:

An agreed extension date. The taxpayer agrees or consents to an extension of the limitation period on IRS form 872. A taxpayer may agree to an extension when negotiating with the IRS and there is less than 180 days left before the expiration of the limitation period. If the taxpayer does not agree to an extension, the IRS will issue a notice of deficiency to protect the running of the statute of limitations against the IRS.

Limitation period increased to 6 years. If the original return as filed, omitted gross income that exceeds 25% of the gross income that was stated on the filed return the limitation period is increased. In this case, the three-year limitation period is replaced with a six-year limitation period.

Unlimited period. If the original return was never filed or is filed fraudulently with the intent to evade tax, there is an unlimited statute of limitations period. If the IRS claims fraud, you must refute the allegation; else there is no limit as to how long the IRS can come after you.

Notice of Deficiency Extension. When the IRS mail a Notice of Deficiency, the period of limitations is suspended for the period during which the IRS is precluded from assessing the tax, plus 60 days.

Collection

Different from assessment is collection activity. Collection refers the time that the IRS has to implement administrative means to collect back taxes. This can get a little complex. Hang in there, and it should become a less confusing in the following paragraphs.

Ten Year Rule on Collections

The IRS has 10 years to collect unpaid taxes before the statue limitation period expires. Note that the 10 year period begins to run only after an assessment of tax has been made (See the assessment paragraphs, above). To put this into perspective, the IRS has three years to make an assessment and then an additional ten years to collect the tax.

Case Study

Geoff and Arlene filed their 2011 tax return. They had operated a small business and claimed losses from the operation of the business on their return. In 2014, the IRS audited their 2011 return. Certain losses were disallowed, and the IRS made an assessment of additional tax of $12000 in 2014. The IRS can collect the unpaid tax by levy until 2024.

Court Action May Extend the Limitation Periods

The IRS has more than ten ways to go to court to aid in the collection of tax debt. When a judgment is obtained, it is not subject to a time limitation and may be collected upon *at any time*. For example the IRS can institute suit for the foreclosure of real property (lien foreclosure) or it could take a judgment against you and execute on the judgment against assets.

Fraudulent Conveyance

The IRS can bring suit to set aside a conveyance to a third person. A fraudulent conveyance is a transfer of title or interest in real or personal property to avoid tax payment of a properly assessed tax. For example, if you had sold your 1965 Shelby Mustang to your brother-in-law for $100, the IRS would claim that you made a transfer for less than the fair market value of the car, solely for the purpose of avoiding your tax obligation. The IRS can bring suit to have the transfer of the car set aside, then seize and sell the Mustang. The proceeds of the sale will be applied to your tax debt.

Summary of Statute of Limitations

The statue limitations may prevent the IRS from collecting from you because too much time has passed. However, there are many, many exceptions that extend the periods of limitation. Remember that the basic limitation period is three years to make an assessment of the tax and then 10 years additional from the date of assessment to collect the unpaid tax.

CHAPTER TWENTY-ONE

BANKRUPTCY TO REDUCE TAX DEBT

An Important Tool for IRS Debt

Bankruptcy can be an important tool in the case of larger old tax debt. However, contrary to what some who advertise on day time TV imply, bankruptcy will not discharge all tax debt for the average person.

Discharge of tax debt under both Chapter 7 and Chapter 13 of the bankruptcy code is permitted under a limited set of circumstances. Bankruptcy law is complicated enough that it trips up lawyers. The best that can be done here is a superficial treatment of the main points. Hopefully, this will be enough to give you some understanding of the interplay between tax law and bankruptcy law.

The overarching goal of bankruptcy is a "fresh start". The general idea is that if a person is insolvent, she may be relieved of debts through bankruptcy. In passing bankruptcy laws, Congress attempts to strike a balance between the impossibility of paying all of the debts that a person may owe and the rights of creditors, including the IRS.

Priorities

Some creditors have priority in claiming money or assets from the bankrupt estate. Said another way, some creditors have an interest in the property in the possession of the bankrupt and may have rights to the secured property or have other statutory priorities. Think of it this way, creditors having priorities go to the head of the line ahead of creditors not having security interests or priorities. IRS tax liens tax liens arising from properly assessed taxes have priority.

The Bankruptcy Code slices and dices the various priorities in more detail than can be covered here. For income tax purposes, the following rules will apply to most individuals:

- The due date for filing a tax return is at least three years ago;
- The tax return was filed at least two years ago;
- The tax was assessed at least 240 days ago;
- The tax return was not fraudulent; and,
- The taxpayer is not guilty of tax evasion.

Provide Copies of Tax Returns to Court

Each item in the above list must be met for a tax debt to be discharged. In addition, a bankruptcy trustee will require petitioners to provide a copy of the most recent tax return to the court and prove that the four previous tax return years have been filed. If not filed, the petitioner will have to prepare the returns and file them before the first meeting of creditors.

As you can see the ability to discharge past-due taxes is very powerful and can be of great benefit to you. However, you can also note that the technical requirements prevent you from discharging any tax debt that is recent or for years for which you have not filed a tax return. It might be helpful to think of it this way: old tax debt for which a tax return was filed when due may have a chance to be discharged through bankruptcy.

– Think twice, if the main reason to file bankruptcy is tax debt

If the only reason that you are considering bankruptcy is IRS tax debt, be especially cautious. A paralegal at the bankruptcy law firm is not qualified to give you advice on this subject. The dischargeability of tax debt is often confused, even for lawyers. It is a real tragedy when I speak with someone who filed bankruptcy and came out of the bankruptcy still owing all of their tax debt and did not receive any real benfit from having filed.

CHAPTER TWENTY-TWO

TAX PAYER ADVOCATE

The Taxpayer Advocate Service (TAS) is an independent organization within the IRS. TAS is under the supervision and direction of the Taxpayer Advocate, who is appointed by and reports directly to the Commissioner of Internal Revenue.

TAS can help you resolve your problems with the IRS if:

- Your problem is causing financial difficulty for you;
- You face an immediate threat of adverse action; or,
- You have tried repeatedly to contact the IRS but no one has responded.

TAS assistance is not given in every case. If TAS accepts your case you will receive personalized service from a knowledgeable taxpayer advocate who will listen to your problem and help you understand what needs to be done to resolve the problem. The advocate will be your point of contact until the problem is resolved or it determined that no further assistance can be given.

Eligibility

You must meet certain eligibility requirements before TAS will accept your matter for assistance. In general, TAS will not assist in cases involving the processing original tax returns, amended returns, rejected returns and injured spouse claims. TAS may be able to help in situations where there is some financial difficulty or emergency or hardship that can be relieved if the IRS acts more quickly than its normal procedures would allow.

How TAS may Be Able to Help

Where eligibility is established and your case is accepted, TAS acts as an "expeditor" to connect you with a responsible person within the IRS. The objective is to help move your case along. Other examples of where the TAS may be helpful are where a taxpayer has tried to resolve a problem through normal IRS channels and those channels have broken down; or, where the taxpayer has some unique factor or issue and the IRS is applying a one-size-fits-all approach.

TAS has many advocates geographically located in cities around the country, and the service is free. In addition, advocates may connect with you over the Internet using a video conference technology. To apply for TAS assistance telephone (877) 777-4778 or fill out IRS form 911 "Request for Taxpayer Advocate Service Assistance".

When TAS Cannot Help

It is best to think of the TAS as a means of coordinating communications with the IRS. The TAS will reject any request for assistance that involves questions of the constitutionality of the tax system; or where the taxpayer is motivated solely for frivolous delay of IRS enforcement; or, to avoid filing a return or paying of federal taxes.

TAS can do almost anything to help with a taxpayer's hardship. But, it can only require the IRS to take actions within the IRS's normal power. For example, a taxpayer cannot use TAS to dispute the merits of a previously assessed tax liability.

No Confidentiality with TAS

There are two things to keep in mind. The taxpayer advocate is not bound by any confidentiality. What you say to the advocate may be repeated and disclosed to an IRS agent. The advocate has complete discretion to share and disclose whatever you say to the IRS and has no duty to keep your communication confidential. Obvious, but worth mentioning here, is that there is no attorney-client privilege between the Advocate's office and the taxpayer.

CHAPTER TWENTY-THREE

IDENTITY THEFT

Identity theft is a fact of life, and it happens with tax returns and refunds. It can happen when someone files a tax return using someone else's identity and claims tax refunds using names and social security numbers stolen from other taxpayers. This is a crime.

According to the IRS, the most common fraudulent refund checks that check cashiers will see are U.S. Treasury refund checks and bank checks, as for instance a check from a tax refund anticipation loan. The are checks made payable to the taxpayer whose identity has been stolen and cashed by the criminals.

IRS Position on Identity Theft

The IRS takes identity theft seriously. The fraudulently cashing of, or the obtaining of a tax refund through identity theft has become a major issues for the government. The IRS is vigorously prosecuting persons and groups that participate in these schemes. A common thread is that the return is filed with a stolen identity, but the refund address is a mail drop address to which the criminals have access. More sophisticated schemes involving opening bank accounts using false identification, and then have refund checks sent for direct deposit into the account. As soon as the refund is deposited, the criminals drain all of the money out of the account and disappear. This is a problem for you because the IRS will initially believe that you filed the fraudulent return.

Beware of Suspicious Activity

You need to know, that the IRS will never initiate contact with a taxpayer by email, Facebook or other social media to request your financial information. IRS employees are prohibited from using email to contact taxpayers. The IRS never sends an email to tell you that you are being audited or that you will receive a refund. If you are contacted in any of these ways, it is likely a fraudulent attempt to obtain your personal information.

Someone Else Used Your Child's SSAN

Another way that identity theft and fraudulent refunds occur is when someone else files a tax return using your child's social security number. Using your child's SSAN the, criminals will claim that child as a dependent. They will likely claim earned income credits, child tax credits or child care credits to increase the refund. If it happens, your e-filed tax return will be rejected because your child's social security number has already been used by someone else.

If you discover identity theft with regard to your taxes there is a remedy. In the case where your child's SSAN has been used, you will need to file your tax return by printing it to paper and mailing it to the IRS (the old-fashioned way, with the stamp). In about six weeks the IRS will contact you. Provide the information requested.

Sometimes the above scenario happens when a divorced spouse or relative claims the dependent child on his or her own tax return. This is not identity theft. However follow the same procedure (print and mail your return). When you are contacted, you may need to show that the child lived with you and that you provided more than ½ of the child's support for the year. There may be some other questions but be assured that most people usually do not have a problem providing the information. The IRS will contact the other person, adjust their return and collect from that person the wrongfully obtained portion of the refund they received.

Identity Theft Affidavit

If your identity has been taken and used for a tax return you should immediately contact the IRS. You will be required to complete form 14039 "Identity Theft Affidavit". If your wallet was stolen or there's some other theft of personal information, it is helpful to the IRS to attach to the affidavit a copy of the police report.

ABOUT THE AUTHOR

The main reason that people get into serious tax difficulty is because they ignore the problem until it grows and grows until it is over-whelming. *Back Taxes & Tax Debt* is a book to help people resolve their own tax problems. Even after the tax problem has gotten so serious that you need to hire a tax attorney, this book will be enormously helpful to an understanding of how your case is progressing.

Mr. Lowrey is an attorney and represents clients in federal tax collection and tax controversy cases nationwide. He is the founder of TaxLawyerOnline™, a virtual law firm delivering legal services online to clients anywhere, at any time. *e*Lawyering is doing legal work – not just marketing – over the Web.

He resides in Las Vegas Nevada with his wife and their golden retriever, Flap Jacks.

Thank you for your interest. It is my sincere hope that you have found this book helpful in your tax matter.

Sincerely,

Donald E. Lowrey, JD LLM

Tax **Lawyer** Online™

Attorney tax help and assistance <u>online</u>

A virtual law firm, providing
Services online on <u>your</u> schedule.

Before work, after work or when the kids
are in bed. - Convenience 24/7.

We help people just like you.
Tax problems are complicated,
We make it look easy.

Stop Worrying,
Get Started Now

<u>www.taxlawyeronline.net</u>

www.ingramcontent.com/pod-product-compliance
Lightning Source LLC
Chambersburg PA
CBHW031944190326
41519CB00007B/654